WHEN
THE
LIGHTS
GO
OUT

WHEN THE LIGHTS GO OUT

FROM SURVIVOR TO CHAMPION

DAVID RODRIGUEZ

Published 2016

Printed in the United States of America
ISBN: 978-0-9983080-0-5
E-ISBN: 978-0-9983080-1-2
Library of Congress Control Number: 2016918046

Cover and interior design by Tabitha Lahr

Find the author online at DavidNinoRodriguez.com.

The author has changed some names, places, and recognizable details to protect the privacy of friends and family members mentioned in the book.

"It is not the critic who counts; not the man who points out how the strong man stumbles, or where the doer of deeds could have done them better.

The credit belongs to the man who is actually in the arena, whose face is marred by dust and sweat and blood; who strives valiantly; who at the best knows in the end the triumph of high achievement, and who at the worst, if he fails, at least fails while daring greatly."

—Theodore Roosevelt

To my beautiful mother.

Contents

BACKGROUND

David Rodriguez was formerly ranked, with impeccable titles and glory, as a six-time champion and heavyweight boxer. He carries an impressive 37-2 record, including 35 explosive knockouts (25 in the first round). David shares story after story of how to adapt a mindset to help you liberate yourself what you may feel stuck in. He delivers his talks with an entertaining, uplifting, no-holds-barred attitude. He shares the lessons, discipline, and dedication it takes to be number one in the face of life's curves.

David's interest in boxing began at the young age of five. He was bullied and teased as a child. Not fitting in, he was often labeled as an outcast, and ultimately placed in an alternative school as a troubled teenager. He shares stories of how his closest friends were part of the troublemaking group he met "in the principal's office." It took mentoring, belief, and a strict persistence to fuel his drive and determination through his journey and life of boxing.

David turned professional at the young age of twenty-one and quickly drew attention, buzz, and praise in the ring. He learned how to channel his aggression and passion into something greater than himself. He experienced two near-death episodes in 2011 which altered his life and boxing career permanently. He experienced severe heartache with the sudden loss of his dear older sister from cirrhosis of the liver in 2009. He has also experienced disappointment and corruption, leading to the severance from his longtime and once-trusted management team in 2011. People instantly connect with David's humility, humor, inspiration, and triumph over adversity with his ability to start over and create the life he was destined for.

"When you find yourself in the depths of hell, look up, for even the act of doing so will let Satan know he has no power over your soul."

—David Rodriguez

CHAPTER 1

SCARRED FOR LIFE

I have just been murdered.

At least, the realization has just set in that I have been murdered.

It is 2:30 in the morning on a cold and disorienting night in Scottsdale, Arizona, in late December. The events play as flashes, permanently leaving an imprint on my confused and desperate mind. I'm strapped to a gurney in an ambulance, with a team of frantic paramedics covered in blood all around me. I feel sorrow and desperation as my life starts slipping away. I have just been on the receiving end of a brutal and extremely violent knife attack to the left side of my throat and face. I'm lying on the gurney, motionless, with an open gash that runs from my ear along the jawline to the bottom of my lip. My throat is only holding onto my face by strings of skin and tissue. I lie still, my life in jeopardy. My throat is torn open and exposed. I'm gasping for any last bit of oxygen I can inhale while the blood fills my esophagus. I can feel and hear my heartbeat slowing down, wanting to come to a halt. My life's blood keeps gushing out of my throat, pouring onto my cold, bare chest.

The paramedics are screaming for me to stay awake, but the voices start to fade as I begin my journey into the great abyss. The understanding that I have just been murdered sends a shot of adrenaline throughout my body. Tears start to swell and flow down my cheeks as I realize I will never see my family again. I feel a warm sensation come over me as I send small prayers of goodbye to each of my family members. The acceptance starts to creep into my confused mind and fading life. Thoughts rush into my head as I start to comprehend my death.

I keep seeing myself as a little boy. Events of my life start to unravel as I gasp for the last remaining air I can endure. I glance to my left and notice a shadow in human form start to engulf my body. I lie there calmly as it grows and engulfs the inside of the ambulance. As I feel it grow, I start to lose resistance while my consciousness slips away.

I am immediately jolted back to a simpler time in life. It was a moment in time that seems like yesterday. I see myself as a child. I'm no longer gasping for air or in any kind of pain. I'm now observing moments of my childhood. I begin to recognize and feel every emotion as if I'm viewing it from the Rolodex of my memory. I'm ushered back, remembering where it all began, and start to get an understanding about the reasons why. I'm now staring back in confused observation to the summer of 1982. Then, I was at the impressionable and delicate age of five, living on the far east side of El Paso, Texas. I can see my five-year-old frame all over again. I get an epiphany about why I've endeavored all my life to be a boxer. It began with a childhood of emotional insecurity and fear. Growing up, I had a wonderful home life with a loving family, but one experience in particular was the catalyst that led me into a lifetime of frustration, insecurity, and chaos. It would be the jumpstart that would eventually lead me into the long and crazy roller coaster of a ride in the boxing world, transforming me into a killer in the ring with no mercy or sympathy for any rival I would later face down.

My experiences of being bullied started at very young age. I was a small kid, outgoing and happy for the most part. I went to the playground next to my house like every kid would do in those days, with a big smile on my face and the whole world to explore, no inkling of wrongdoing, and the naive sense that no one could do harm to me. I had a loving family with two older sisters who were highly protective of me. The world was a magical place and I had no comprehension of hurt and pain, except maybe the temper tantrums I threw when I didn't get the toy I wanted. I was an innocent kid, oblivious to the ways of the world. I can remember walking to the playground when I was six years old, with the bright sunshine beaming on my face, not a care in the world. Life was fantastic. I would show up every day to meet with my neighborhood playmates. We'd slide down the slide and then run over to jump on the merry-go-round. Back then, we didn't have the worries and paranoia that kids have today. The world seemed like a much safer place. It wasn't out of the ordinary to go to friends' houses and raid the fridge or stay for dinner, just so long we were back before it was dark and before the street lights came on.

That's the way life was in the early 1980s. Every day was a social gathering in the neighborhoods. There were no iPhones or Internet. Television was limited to a few channels and most kids couldn't sit through a single program. Everyone wanted to be outside playing. It's just what we did in those days. If you fell down and got a scratch on your knee or knocked out a tooth playing, it was considered normal and you'd be outside doing it again the very next day. The playground was a place of imagination and adventure. The laughter of children could be heard throughout the neighborhood.

The girls used to play a flirtatious game where they would pick a boy they liked and chase after him until they caught him and dogpiled him. I would spend the first part of the day at the playground running from the girls until I ran out of breath, then get caught, wrestled down, and dogpiled. I'd get up to smile and then go about my activities. This was fun, for a while. The only problem was that one of the girls was about four years older than me and severely obese, which made me run like hell from her in the hope that she wouldn't be the first one to catch me and slam me to the ground. She probably had a crush on me, because when I showed up at the park she would lock eyes with me like a pitbull, point, and yell, "Get David!" That was my signal to run as fast as my little legs could carry me.

This would-be harmless game got old fast, so I decided to stick up for myself. I decided to walk up to her and tell her that I didn't appreciate her grabbing me every day and throwing me to the ground. The day came that I finally built up the courage to tell her that I'd had enough. I showed up to the park that day with my chest popped out and chin held high as I approached her. I went up to her before she could yell out my name and said, "No more, Angel!" Yes, her name was Angel.

I remember the proud and cocky feeling I had after I said those bold and brave words and watched the tears well up in her eyes. After that, life went in slow motion. She reached out and grabbed me, threw me onto the ground, then kicked me in the testicles and punched me repeatedly in the face. I remember all the kids circling around us and the embarrassment I felt. She was too heavy for me to push her off of me, so I played possum until she got tired and out of breath. I stood up while the kids' screams and laughter deafened my ears. I wiped the blood from my nose and mouth. My head hung low as I took the long walk back home.

The guilt, humility, and shame hung over me as I entered my house. My parents looked at me when I got home that afternoon.

"What happened?" they asked, clearly concerned.

"I fell off the swing set," I said, looking at the floor. I knew deep down they didn't believe me. A kid who falls off a swing set doesn't begin to cry and then lock himself in his room. I knew they were skeptical, but telling my father a girl beat me up at the playground would be too humiliating.

After weeks went by of hiding and being a recluse, I decided to return to the playground, hoping that everyone would have forgotten and my life could resume as normal. This wasn't the case. I ended up becoming the kid who played alone while the other kids laughed, pointed fingers at me, and chuckled. This went on for weeks. It got to the point where Angel would come by and punch me in the arm occasionally to show her dominance and authority. I went from the once-popular kid on the playground to a loner, and it was devastating.

After coming home for several weeks depressed and distant, my family knew the jig was up. I had gone from a happy-go-lucky kid to a distant, depressed recluse who locked himself in his room for hours. This is where having an overprotective mother and two older sisters, not to mention a strong, macho, alpha-male father, worked to my benefit. Although I wanted no help, they had other plans in mind. One day as I got on my bike to ride to the playground they formulated a secret plan to follow me. I, of course, would have been humiliated if I'd known. As I got to the playground, completely oblivious to their plans, the harassment started. A few kids were laughing at me and poking fun, but today would prove to be different. Today, Angel decided to get bolder than usual. She came up and pretended to punch me. I flinched and she laughed, punching me in the arm and stomach as the other kids circled around me in laughter. Well, to my surprise, that would be the last time she ever did that again.

My mother and sisters ran to my aid. The words my mother and sisters used toward this girl were terrifying. I had never seen such anger. They made the girl apologize to me and the rest of the children. After the apology, Angel took off running home, screaming and crying.

My mother grabbed me by the hand and said, "I'm taking you home to your father! No son of mine is going to be picked on like this."

As I made my way home I was traumatized and shocked at what had just occurred, and the scariest part was yet to come. Having to explain to my father that a little girl kicked my ass every day was going to be humiliating and dreadful. I parked my Huffy bicycle in front of the house and walked inside. The front door slammed behind me under the saddening stares of my sisters and mother. I was escorted into the kitchen and saw my father staring at me with concern and disappointment. His hands were folded behind his head as he leaned back in the kitchen chair with his feet up on the table.

"You wanna start from the beginning and tell me how this all happened?"

I had nothing to say. I just hung my head low in shame. My father stood up and knelt down beside me as he put his arms around me. This was a completely different response from what I had been expecting to get. He spoke to me calmly but sternly and said he had just the right idea for me.

"Do you love the movie *Rocky*?" he asked.

I looked up and smiled because he knew it was my favorite movie ever. He asked me if I would like to learn how to box. I was confused. From what I saw in the movies, it seemed like gory and horrible punishment.

He said, "I'm going to call your Uncle Tom and get you started. He trains the Fort Bliss Army team."

I was petrified. *I can't even beat up a girl, yet this madman wants to turn me into Rocky? Is he insane? Has he lost his mind?* Less than ten minutes later, he was on the phone having a talk with my so-called Uncle Tom, whom I'd never met. All I could hear was him chuckling and laughing as he told Tom the story.

At the end of the phone call he said, "I'll bring him by the gym at the end of the week, Tom!"

These were the fateful words I didn't want to hear. I was six years old, for God's sake! I didn't want to go to a bloody boxing gym and get beat up like Rocky! I wanted to stay home and play with my action figures and ride my bike. I thought I would be catered to and cared for. I wanted people to feel sorry for me. I wanted to play the sympathy card. I went to bed every night that week petrified out of my mind that I was going to go to the gym and get beat up like Rocky. Every night before bed I kept imagining his bloody face, with thoughts of when he fought Apollo and his famous, "Yo, Adrian, I did it!"

Finally the day came. It was Friday morning and my father walked into my room to wake me up, a big grin on his face, with the comment, "Are you ready to learn how to defend yourself?"

I rolled out of bed with a faint nod and said, "Okay, Daddy."

He fed me a healthy breakfast, grabbed me by the hand, and walked me to his big blue Cadillac parked in the driveway. I glanced back at my toys, wanting nothing more than to run to them and act like a kid. The walk to his car was like the green mile. I felt I was being punished for being a coward and that I'd be sacrificed to the boxing world. All of this just seemed so premature and ridiculous to a little kid my age. Now, looking back, I see my dad's actions were tough love and I wouldn't change things for the world. My father knew best and he would show it in his own tough but caring way.

As I got in the car and shut the door, he slapped his heavy hand on the top of my head, where I could feel his hard gold ring against my scalp. I generally got mad when he did that because it would leave a knot on the top of my head almost every time. This time was an exception. I knew it was a small price to pay for him to smile and take me to regain the dignity and self-respect that I had lost. My father was about to initiate his son, and lead me down a road that would eventually transform me into a world contender and champion prize fighter.

CHAPTER 2

INTO THE BELLY OF THE BEAST

David Rodriguez, five years old

David Rodriguez with mother

I don't know what was worse, the long drive to my crucifixion or that the Golden Oldies my father loved were playing on the AM station the whole way. Either way, it was torturous. Maybe the drive into the poor side of town, or what today we would call the ghetto, together with the songs of John Denver playing in my ears, made my stomach curdle. I was a child and I knew it wasn't fitting for me to roll up to a boxing gym blasting John Denver's and Neil Diamond's greatest hits. Of course when we arrived at the gym, all the tough little Mexicans were staring at me, smirks on their faces. They looked at me like fresh meat. Another little white kid trying to prove himself, but once he gets a bloody nose, he'll run right back, crying to his parents.

As my dad took me out of the car, holding my hand as we walked into the gym, I stared up at him, wondering if he would stick up for me if someone approached me. I remember the smell of canvas and leather, along with the singing beats of a speed bag in perfect rhythm. I gazed around the gym, holding my father's hand tightly while observing the kids punching the heavy bags, making tough, gritty, groaning sounds. I noticed all the old boxing fight posters coming off the walls, held in place with one last piece of dingy yellow tape.

There were two young boys my age sparring in the ring. They were punching the hell out of each other and bleeding all over one another. It looked like a dogfight. I went to grip my father's hand tighter, but all I grabbed was air. I looked up and he was gone. I looked around in a panic. How could my father, who loved me so much, bring me here and forsake me so treasonously? What should I do now? I looked around frantically, and the walls started to close in on me. I started feeling dizzy. I couldn't breathe. My lungs started feeling tight while my knees began to shake and my palms became clammy with sweat. In prison terms, I was the new fresh fish and everybody knew it. Attention started to gravitate toward me. As my breath became more and more shallow, I started looking for the exit. Tears started welling up in my eyes as panic overtook my nervous system. I wanted to faint. I started to quietly shuffle backwards and make my way out to the door. As I inched toward it I could sense my freedom drawing closer and closer. I wanted the heck out of there, and my game plan was to run to the first pay phone I saw and call my mom. I would explain what an evil deed my dad had done, and he would hear it from her as she drove one hundred miles per hour to save her only son. I had the escape plan all figured out.

I was no more than two feet away from the door, nearly home free, when I heard, "Hey kid! Where ya going?" I froze once again. I slowly turned around and saw an older, nervous-looking man with an extremely high and intense energy approaching me. He had an obnoxious smile and a nervous chatter in his teeth. He looked about fifty-five or sixty years old.

He walked toward me and said, "No-no-no, you're not going anywhere, kid!"

I stood in shock, trying to figure this man out. He grabbed my arm firmly and turned me away from the door and back into the direction of the gym. He yelled out to the other coaches, "Hey everybody, this is David Rodriguez's kid! Little Davy!"

As if this day couldn't get any worse, it just did. He scooted me away from the entrance and all the other kids and put me in front of the shadowboxing mirror. He started making grunts and groans while he shadowboxed in front of me. I thought this man was completely nuts. He proceeded to show me how to stand in a fighting stance in front of that mirror, with my hands up and legs slightly bent. He then showed me how to throw my little fists out as I turned my waist. I could tell I looked ridiculous, but I was too scared not to do as I was told. During these movements my eyes would occasionally wander into the ring where the more advanced kids were. I looked in awe as they bloodied each other up and fought without an ounce of fear. I couldn't believe kids my age could do such a thing. How did they grow up so much tougher than me? How could they be six to ten years old and fight like grown men?

As I stayed busy with the repetitive boredom of doing the same moves in front of the mirror, Tom went off to get the hand pads, or mitts as we called them. He returned with that same nervous energy and began to teach me the brutal art and the sweet science of boxing. He tucked my chin down and showed me how to throw a proper jab. Then a right hand. I would mess up continuously, but he would shrug it off with his nervous laughter and chattering teeth, only to show me again. Every time he smiled, I could see every vein in his neck tense up as he clenched his jaw. He had this nervous habit from the first day I met him, and as of the writing of this book, he still does.

Tom had a knack for talking so fast that I got the impression he was auctioning off whatever subject he was talking about. I used to see if I could count how many times he gasped for air between sentences. I swear that most times I could never even begin a count. It was dizzying. A person could go into a hypnotic trance just listening to this man race through sentences. I believe that he missed his calling and should have been an auctioneer or horse-racing commentator.

As the hours went on at the gym, he started to see that I liked to curve my jab and come up with my legs. He took a few steps back and said, "This kid wants to learn how to throw the hook, huh?"

I had no idea what the hell a hook was. I didn't know the difference between a left hook and a fish hook. The first thing he ever said about my effort throwing a left hook was, "Son, never hook with a hooker or go out with a hooker. They're both deadly and will ruin you!" I had no idea what the old man was babbling about, so like most people, I just agreed with him to weather the storm of conversation. From that day forward I learned to never ask questions and just agree with him, because his answers were so long and continuous. A nod in agreement or an "okay" worked best.

After hours of working out, he couldn't believe the energy I had. I wanted to keep going. I even developed my own sound effects for all of my punches. After what seemed like hours, my father walked through the door with a huge grin. I ran toward him in hopes of telling him everything I had learned. He laughed and with his continuous big grin he showed me exactly where he had been hiding and watching the whole time. My dad didn't forsake me. He was watching his boy the entire time! He wanted to watch his son develop confidence. He wanted his son to fend for himself but never left him. He knew it was something I had to be alone to do. My sweet, dear old dad had a method to his madness.

CHAPTER 3

SCHOOL CONFESSIONS

After a short while I was a regular at the boxing gym. I became friends with most of the kids there and it evolved into a kind of day care for me. I was there almost every day, learning how to punch correctly and protect myself. My parents decided that, instead of letting me deal with more humiliation from the kids from the playground that would have gone to the same school as me, they wanted me to attend a Catholic school and grow closer to God. They had me enrolled at St. Patrick's elementary school.

When I entered the school, all the teachers were astonished at how fast I could read and comprehend the subject matter. I never stumbled on any words and reading was a breeze for me. I owe that major advancement in schooling to my mother. I had learned how to read by the beginning of kindergarten. It was a daily routine in my household to have my mother wrestle me down as I threw temper tantrums at the dining room table, where she would teach me how to read. It was agonizing to a child my age. She literally made me learn to read by sounding out the words and learning the vowels. In no time she had me reading novels. By the time I entered school I was way ahead of any of my classmates. It wasn't even close. What my parents didn't bargain for was that being so advanced in my reading level would make class agonizingly boring for me. I was reading at a college level by the time I was in third grade. I would always be picked at least twice a week to serve as an altar boy in mass and as the main reader. I was honored by this, but it didn't cure my painful boredom in school. This boredom led me into a world of trouble—manipulative and sinister trouble. I had to get my stimulation from somewhere and the classroom wasn't providing me with that. I can still remember waiting for the other children to painfully sound out the words they were reading out loud. They could barely read any paragraphs at a third or fourth grade level. I was already breezing through *National Geographic* magazines and encyclopedias. My mother would make me read the *New York Times* or *Wall Street Journal* every morning in the car on the way to school. She had me reading on subjects like politics and economics.

Although she thought this was all benefitting me, it was the perfect recipe to make me become the class clown. Every day, church and school was driving me insane. I felt like an institutionalized, mindless drone, and this led to a part-time hobby as a creative prankster. It wasn't before long that my teachers became the target of my pranks. I never woke up excited to go to school to learn—I woke up excited only to go off to school in order to pull another mean and distasteful prank on the teacher of my choosing. I really never wanted to cause any harm, I just wanted some innocent fun and cheap stimulation. I had many practical jokes and always had a smart-ass response, but this escalated to my favorite prank, which was to hand-deliver fresh dog crap to the inside of my teacher's lunch bag in the mornings. I would patiently wait until lunchtime to see her face and hear the yell of horror when she opened her sandwich bag to find a fresh dog turd nestled inside the sandwich. I am thankful to this day that they never took a bite of my shit sandwich creation. The odor always gave it away.

After spending most my days of getting caught and sitting in the corner, I realized crime just wasn't paying enough. Not only that, but I was going to confession almost every other week. It got to the point that I was even making up elaborate stories to tell the priest. I soon discovered that didn't help because he just kept giving me more of the rosary to pray. Even the nuns got a piece of the action and would pull out a heavy meter stick or ruler and whack the hell out of my little ass in front of the whole class. Still, I would lift my chin up, wipe away my tears, and walk back to my desk with a chuckle, just waiting to do my cunning little dirty deeds again. Devising my sinister plans was the best part of it all. I sat in class day after day, dreaming of what prank was next and which nun would be on the receiving end.

I was able to maintain this behavior while racing through my chapters and finishing all of my tests first. It was just too easy for me. School was boring, but being a part-time asshole never got old. It wasn't irregular for me to do most of my school work in the principal's office. I actually enjoyed it more because I loved making the receptionist and principal laugh with my fart noises and snoring sounds. I had a way of making people enjoy my juvenile behavior. Every time the teacher sent me to the principal's office, I gladly went, with my notebook in hand, pencil in my ear, and a huge shit-eating grin on my face. I had the luxury of this routine for a few years, until I had had enough.

I was in sixth grade and I knew the nightmare of Cathedral would begin next year. Cathedral was an all-boys middle and high school. I wanted no part of that. The other kids seemed so excited, but going to an all-boys school during my developing years sounded like a living hell. I was just a young boy but I discovered girls quite early. There was no way in hell that I would go to an all-boys high school—at least, not if I could help it. So I decided it was time to ramp up my bullshit troublemaking skills and get my little ass kicked out. My parents refused to take me out of Catholic school and nobody listened to me when I said I didn't want to be there. Although all my good buddies would be at Cathedral, it still wasn't enough to keep me from wanting to go to a coed school instead. I had to escape from this prison so I could meet girls the next coming year. I was not going to spend my first kissing and experimenting days at an all-boys school.

I began to formulate my plan. A filthy and nasty one at that. My parents didn't want to listen to me? Fine. Let me do one final prank to get my ass booted out. I needed the proper tools for my prank. I decided I was going to need a good bag of dog shit, some gift wrapping paper and a cake for Miss Smith's birthday. (I won't reveal her real name for obvious reasons.) She celebrated her birthday every year by opening ass-kissing gifts from students. Every year the kids would bring her unique gifts in hopes of being the new teacher's pet. I mean, these kids really kissed her ass. Kids would bring her the biggest and most expensive presents as if they were trying to compete with all three of the wise men in the manger scene with Jesus. I decided that this time I was going to out-do them all, and do it in spectacular fashion.

So, the day before her birthday I decided to surprise my dad and clean the dog crap in the backyard like a good son—something he usually had to make me do, his reasoning being that the three bulldogs were somehow my fault. In any case, I collected just enough fresh dog treats to fit in a nice elegant box. The box was taken from a sweater my mom bought for me at Dillard's. The next part of my ingenious plan was to go to Radio Shack and buy myself a nice little fuse detonator that would be tied to the top of the box. It had two ends spread apart and when the two ends clapped together, it would ignite a flame that would then hit the wick I would place in the middle of the two ends. The plan was that once she tore off the paper and opened the box, it would snap the wire to the detonator and BLAAAAM! Dog crap should be all over her face and the chalk board. I was never so excited and sure in my entire life. This was going to be the prank of all pranks. The next day couldn't come fast enough.

Finally, the day of reckoning. I carefully placed the dog turds in the box with the nice little detonator hidden and nicely snuggled in the fresh dog excrement. I connected the wire to the detonator and was extremely careful when closing the box and gift-wrapping it with all my love. I used wrapping paper with fireworks on it just for kicks. I wrote a nice, real long card that said, *Have a Happy, Explosive Birthday and let your day be lit up like fireworks on the Fourth of July!* It was perfect.

All night I stared at my creation while imagining the reaction it was going to get. I was about to be a legend for all the classes to come after me. I could hardly sleep that night. When morning came I jumped out of bed and ate my breakfast excitedly. My mother never saw me so happy to go to school. As she gave me a ride to school, she talked with me the whole way and asked me what I could have possibly got the teacher. Those were questions I was not prepared for, so I started making up answers and getting really nervous. My mom always had a sense about me. She knew I was up to no good and I knew the jig was about to be up if I didn't play the game correctly. I said, "Mom, it's just a collage of pictures and art I made in appreciation for Miss Smith." My mom looked at me jigsawed and reluctantly let me out of the car once we arrived in front of the school. I felt her glare like a laser beam as I walked inside the school doors. I carefully walked into the classroom, making sure not to bump the box. I placed the gift that would keep on giving for years to come on her desk carefully.

Miss Smith smiled and said, "Thank you, David, you are so very kind!"

All day I sat and gazed at my shit box, wondering when she would open it. After lunch, the time arrived. It was fourth period and the time to open all the presents had arrived. I raised my hand and asked her if she could open my present last.

She said, "Most certainly!"

After the long process of opening all the presents, she looked at mine. The tension could have been cut with a knife and I started getting nervous and sweating. That was a dead giveaway. She read my card out loud and then glared at me. She must have sensed and felt my nervousness. I tried to smile and look at her, but she kept hesitating. She would confusingly stare at the present and then stare right back at me.

She finally looked up at me one last time and said, "David, since you're so sweet, would you mind opening it for me in front of the class?"

I was in absolute shock. I had no type of diversion or distraction to pull on her. I had no excuse why I couldn't. I just froze up once again. She walked to my desk and gently placed the gift of dog shit on my desk to do the honors. There was no way out of this and I definitely didn't want exploding dog shit all over my face. My prank was about to literally backfire on me.

This was until I heard the sweetest little voice saying, "I'll open it!" It was a girl named Sarah, who I was in puppy love with for the few years I went to that school. So now I was in the most awkward and difficult situation of my young life. I either give it to her to open, open it myself, or throw the box out the window. I had to think fast, but I wasn't about to let my schoolboy crush remember me as the guy who got dog crap all over her. So, I decided to do what any real man would do in that situation.

I handed it over to the desk next to me and said, "This is no fun for me because I already know what's in it."

The desk next to me had the quiet kid, the kid that constantly told on me for misbehaving. He looked up with a smile and dug right into the wrapping paper. I sat back and watched with a defiant and evil grin. I was just seconds away from sealing my legacy. Eons passed before he finally got to the point where he could open the box.

Drumroll please. NOTHING. Nothing. Not a damn thing happened. No bang and no flying dog shit. He just looked up and said "It just smells really bad, Miss Smith."

My jaw dropped in disappointment. It was a dud? How could this be? I had practiced with decoys for days! The teacher walked up to the box and peeked inside.

She saw the smelly dog treats I had waiting for her and said, "Dog poo, again, David? Are you running out of ideas?"

I looked down and said, "Well, it was supposed to blow up in your face."

She laughed at me, walked to her desk, and wrote a referral for me to go to the office. She handed it to me. I grabbed the referral and made my way down the hall to the principal's office. I walked slowly. I was frustrated that my plan didn't go accordingly. Then, as I was about to turn the last corner to the next stretch of hallway, I heard a BANG! BANG BANG

BANG! And then shouts as the class came pouring out of the classroom with dog excrement in their hair, faces and clothes. Some of the kids were even slipping and sliding in the hallway trying to work their way frantically to the restroom. Kids looked at me in absolute horror. At that point I knew that this was definitely my last day in Catholic school, and my nightmares of an all-boys school were finally over. I went to the office with bravado and pride. I got lectured and screamed at for the good part of an hour until they could get my mother to leave from work and pick me up.

They kicked me out so fast that this time there was no seeing the Father for a confession. I ended up finding out later that, somehow or another, when all the kids lined up for the water break, they had lined up next to the box. There was a delayed reaction and the box blew up all over about five of my classmates. This certainly did not go as planned, but in the end, my wish had been granted. I got kicked out for good, and I could now go to a regular school.

I went home with a grin, except this time, when I got home, my father didn't have a fun bonding experience for me. He had a nice leather belt that he smacked against his palm, with an *I'm-gonna-whoop-your-ass* look all over his face. He grabbed me and beat my little ass 'til I was black and blue. I was grounded and not allowed to eat dinner with the family. I had to stay in my room and use bags of ice on my butt cheeks as pillows. I couldn't lie down or sit down for days after that incident. That wasn't considered child abuse in those days. It was a good old-fashioned ass beating to discipline a child. I met my goal of getting kicked out of school, but there was a hefty price to pay for it.

CHAPTER 4

SNUFF THE ROOSTER

They say to be careful what you wish for, because you just might get it. Well, after dealing with the physical pain my father inflicted on my butt cheeks, everything was going as planned and I was feeling content that my objective had now been achieved. I was excited to start public school in my area and to have a "normal" upbringing. The summer went by fast, and I was usually outside all day or sweating at the boxing gym. I was excelling at boxing so early, and looking so impressive, that the *El Paso Times* even came out and actually did a full front page write-up.

I was riding on confidence, and I was the captain of my ship. I was a young boy who thought he had figured out life; I had found a way to cheat the system to get exactly what I wanted! I was so excited about the girls I would meet the coming year, and I wanted so much to get acquainted with the female body. I went with my buddies from the neighborhood to our secret hideouts and we looked at *Playboy* magazines most of every day in fascination. My hormones were starting to rage and I could not wait to get into junior high with the

First newspaper write-up

little bit of celebrity status that I'd gained through the local newspaper. I expected school would be a breeze and I'd have as many girlfriends as I could handle. I had it all planned out. Public school would be the beginning of my reign as a king and master player of young women. Nothing could stand in my way. I would daydream every day about who my first girlfriend was going to be and who I would have sex with first. I couldn't wait to see all the new girls and fresh faces from the different schools.

Summer had come and gone extremely fast, and I had an absolute blast with all the kids in my neighborhood. Every day was exciting and every morning was the beginning of a new adventure. But one day I was out playing stickball when the lighting bolt struck, and my reality changed forever. I was playing baseball with rocks and a thick tree branch when my parents rolled up in our brown 1970s Jeep, screaming for me to come over. They had an excited look on both of their faces. I was puzzled and asked what was going on. They said eagerly, "We're going to go look at a new house to buy on the west side of town!" I didn't like the sound of that. I reluctantly got in the Jeep with my two sisters and began asking questions like, "What about my friends?" They answered, "You'll just make new ones, David."

This did not sound good by any means. I had spent a lot of time invested in a calculated plan and it was about to all be flushed down the drain. I had built a rapport with all my friends on the east side and I was carrying a little bit of notoriety as a celebrated local boxer. When we pulled up to what would be our new house, my eyes widened. It was gigantic compared to the red-brick house we had on the east side. We spent the entire day looking at this new house, and I spent the time taking in what would be my new surroundings. It was definitely a lot nicer and quieter, with a full stretch of desert terrain behind the backyard for me to play in and explore. I peeked over the backyard fence and saw my first live horny toad lizard race across the desert sand.

I admit that in that moment, I forgot all about girls and spent the rest of the day catching lizards while my parents negotiated over the house. This started not to seem so bad after all. I could always make new friends.

After a few hours of playing in the hot sun and collecting desert critters, I entered back into the enormous house. I heard my father tell the realtor, "We'll take it!"

I was confused. I get no preparation for this? You can buy a house that quickly? Don't you have to go to a bank and fill out a bunch of paperwork? My mother and father then hugged with smiles and excitement. That was the first point in my young life that I had to learn about life's sudden changes and the laws of adapting to new places and people. I was not ready for this.

Within a week we already had movers at our old house moving everything out. A fear of change came over me. I was about to start school in less than a week and I had no idea what school I was going to. I didn't know a soul in the new neighborhood. This all seemed so unfair. I had no plan anymore. I stared longingly out the back window of our family jeep as we pulled out of the driveway of our old house. I watched all my friends from the neighborhood chase us down as they waved good-bye. The house and their faces just kept getting smaller and more distant as we picked up speed. Everything I was familiar with was vanishing.

As we drove away, I looked down at my favorite pet. It wasn't a kid's ordinary pet, although we also had three bulldogs. This was my unique pet. This was my personal little buddy that I loved so very much. I began whispering to him as I began stroking him, telling him everything will be okay. It was my cock. Yes, I had a pet rooster. I bought a baby chick from a buddy a year ago, not knowing it was going to grow into a full blown rooster. I bought it on impulse because I thought it was so cute and snuggly. I thought it was a great investment for my family, because we would be guaranteed eggs for as long as it lived. Well, it laid no eggs and woke everyone up in the morning. My parents hated it, but I loved him. He had attitude, something I admired so much at that age. They let me keep him and he grew into a huge blistering-red rooster that I named Woody.

I'm absolutely sure my neighbors were ecstatic when we moved away because they lodged daily complaints about my rooster. Every morning at about 4 A.M., the rooster would rise and let out a piercing cock-a-doodle-doo that woke up the entire neighborhood. People hated him, and I'm sure they wanted to dispose of him, but I protected my cock with my life. I loved its attitude. He was ready for any challenge and literally walked around the back yard like he owned it. He bossed around three huge bulldogs and never took any type of shit. If he didn't like you, he'd look at you sideways and chase you around the yard trying to strike you and peck you to death. I used to get a kick by bringing my friends over and watching them run for their lives as they screamed and scaled our backyard wall. I thought it was absolutely hilarious.

As we pulled into the new house, the movers were working diligently to get our things in order and move us in. We unpacked all our belongings and I started setting up my new room. It was a spacious house and there was tons of undeveloped desert terrain stretching out on both sides. I knew my pet rooster would be happy in his new environment. I put him out in the backyard with his cage open, so that he could go back and forth as he damn well pleased. That night, I finally settled myself in and began to relax. My mind was full of wonder with what new adventures I might encounter and what kind of new friends I was going to meet. This change wasn't so bad. Things could be worse. I just had to adapt and I'd meet new friends. I finally dozed off smiling, and dreamt all good and positive dreams. I decided the future was going to be full and bright and I was ready to accept the challenge.

The next morning I woke up with vigor, but I had this lingering feeling of being displaced as I looked around my room in the new day. Initially it was awkward, but I decided to take on the day with excitement and get outside to meet new friends. There was something odd, though. I didn't hear my cock crow in the morning as he usually did. He usually woke me up first thing in the morning and got me ready to start my day. I figured he was probably in shock about the new environment, as I was, and needed to lay dormant for a while. I ran to the breakfast table that overlooked the backyard and the desert beyond, then went out in the backyard, yelling for Woody. I saw and heard nothing. This was strange because he always ran over to me demanding attention. Did he decide to go out and explore the desert? He couldn't have just flown away because I didn't think roosters could fly—at least, I had never seen a cock fly. I walked around the yard, wondering where he could have gone. I peered out into the desert landscape, hoping I would see him frolicking around. Could he have been stolen? Who would want to steal a little boy's pet rooster? This was all confusing and seemed so pointless.

As I walked back inside my new house, puzzled and confused, I started to see traces of horror all over our lawn. I saw a bloody wing on one side of the yard and then a bloody leg on the other. As I looked in horror many thoughts ran into my mind. Everything was in slow motion. I started realizing that I was looking at the hideous massacre of my favorite pet. As I looked all over the backyard in hope of finding what was left of my pet cock, I finally felt the final blow. His head and body were covered in blood and ripped to shreds. I fell to my knees and started crying. Who could have done this? How could there be such evil in this world? None of this made any sense. I ran inside and screamed in horror for my mother and father. I needed to be hugged and pampered. I needed some kind of safety from the realization that I no longer had my beloved pet. This was all too much for me to endure.

My father grabbed my hand and walked outside with me. He gasped in horror and just gave a sensitive and sorry look. He said, "Well, looks like you got some cleaning up to do, kid." I was appalled! Why wasn't he hugging me and telling me that things would be okay? He walked back inside and I heard him say under his breath, "I guess that's why I heard those coyotes last night." What coyotes? We have wild coyotes running around out here? Why had nobody told me this information?

In that moment, I accepted my fate. It was my first real taste of loss and change. I had no idea what I was going to do without my morning Woody to wake me up. I spent the rest of the day mourning over my murdered rooster and cleaning up the bloody remains with a rake. I would cry off and on, but looking back I see that that was another demonstration of my father's tough love for me. That was my pet, and whatever happened to it was my responsibility. This was the first degree of change I felt moving into our new house. What was yet to come was much more humiliating and degrading than cleaning up the scraps of my cock. This was just a small taste of the cruelty to come, of how life would be without my pet Woody.

CHAPTER 5

MY FIRST DAY OF PUBLIC HUMILIATION

Splash!!! I'm jolted out of my slumber at 7 A.M. like a defibrillator to the chest. I was lying in bed with my eyes wide open in complete shock as my mother stood over me with an empty glass in her hand. She had just thrown ice water all over me and my bed sheets. She had taken the responsibility of being my crazy Nazi alarm clock. If I didn't hear her voice the first few times, she would fill up a glass with cold water and throw it all over me. I would wake up with adrenaline shooting throughout my body, cursing under my breath. My mother knew it took extreme measures to get my ass out of bed and she gladly accepted the challenge. This new morning ritual would be the first of many. It would prove to be a rigorous routine, like pulling teeth, just to get me up for school.

This particular day marked my first day of public school; I would attend Moorhead Junior High. It was inconveniently zoned between the borders of middle-class El Paso and the lower-income housing projects on the opposite side of the railroad tracks. I had heard a few horror stories of this school, but I just chalked them up to the other kids' fearful paranoia.

I'd heard of the gangs and the constant beatings they delivered to the rich little white kids. It didn't bother me, though. I was under the impression that I was fearless because I was raised on the east side of El Paso. I had been around all of the toughest and roughest kids from the El Paso ghettos. This school was a west side school, and the west side had a soft reputation to the east side kids.

I started to throw my shorts and shoes on, when my mother walked into my room and said, "No, no, no. You're not starting your first day of school like that! Go into the dining room and put on the clothes I bought for you yesterday."

The clothes she had bought for me yesterday? I didn't see any clothes. What was she talking about? I walked into the dining room and sure enough, there on the table were my brand new clothes laid out for me. This presented a minor problem because in private school we always had to wear uniforms. I had no earthly idea what kids wore to be popular. I was always outside playing in my tennis shoes and shorts. I never took into consideration any type of style or fashion. So, I just gave her a defeated glare, shrugged my shoulders and put on the brand new attire that my mother so proudly had bought for me. It was a bright, preppy, red-and-white-striped shirt, with bright red shorts and a leather belt that looped in the front. The shoes were sockless penny loafers with the penny already placed inside the flap in the front. They even squeaked when I walked. I thought that I looked quite dorky. I didn't want to hurt my mother's feelings, so I decided to give it one full day of school to try out my new look; maybe the ladies at school would dig it. But I was going to school as a prime target. I should've just worn a bull's-eye on my back.

Before I could finish my breakfast, I heard a loud honk outside. It was the only friend that I'd made over the last week, and he was waiting in the car with his mother. He lived just down the street from me and was willing to show me the ropes at school. It was his first day in junior high as well and we were both nervous. I ran outside with half a bacon sandwich in my mouth and milk that I had already spilt on my shorts in a hurry. I jumped in the car and gave my friend a high-five. I tried to remain optimistic about my situation, but I couldn't help being nervous.

He turned to me, looked at my outfit, and chuckled, "Bro, where the hell did you buy those clothes?"

"Dude, my mom got them for me. It's just for today. I'll change it up tomorrow." I knew the horror was just about to begin. I could feel it.

The school wasn't too far. It was actually within walking distance, about two miles. As we got closer to the school, driving down the mountain hill, we could see down to the blacktop. It was crowded with kids and I could hear the screams, laughter, and commotion as we approached the drop off. They were already establishing their identities with the groups and cliques they could fit into. I noticed that none of the kids were dressed like me. My new friend and I looked at each other with no clue what to expect. We exited his mother's car and started our long, treacherous walk down the hill to the blacktop. All I could hear is the noise and commotion of a large crowd. It was a surreal experience. Catholic school was nothing like this. Catholic school was a few hundred people at most and everyone blended in with each other in their uniforms. Here, everyone stood out in independence with their cool stylish outfits.

As we walked down into the battle zone, I zeroed in for the kill. I needed to make friends and I needed to be accepted into some type of popular group fast. The last thing I wanted was to be standing alone in my mother's hand-picked outfit with my hands in my pockets. I was completely depending on my new friend to walk up and begin talking to somebody, anybody. I needed some kind of introduction. We made our long tour around the blacktop, and he wasn't talking to a soul. After a few minutes of this, I took the matter into my own hands to initiate conversation. I pointed out a group of kids and said, "Those guys right there?"

He said, "Yeah, I went to school with them."

I decided to go ahead and approach them, but as I drew closer, they clamored closer and closer together. They all stopped talking and looked over at me.

One pointed at me and said, "Look at his nerdy-ass clothes, guys! Ha ha ha!"

They all laughed and pointed. Even the girls standing next to them joined in. My attempt to make friends backfired and I was humiliated. I decided my best bet was to pretend it didn't happen and start walking backwards while nodding my head in agreement. I had a stupid grin on my face and turned the same shade of red as the stripes on my shirt.

My friend also started laughing and said, "See, I told you those clothes looked really stupid, bro." I felt any pretense of coolness I had psyched up for myself trickle out, and now I was walking around the blacktop completely insecure and embarrassed.

In my panic and humiliation, I approached another group of kids that looked promising, and they did the exact same thing. They turned their backs on me and began laughing. My first day at public school was a living nightmare of evil laughter from the start. I walked away from the crowds of children and decided to seclude myself to avoid further embarrassment. Then I could at least figure out a new plan of attack. I tucked my tail between my legs and took the long retreat over to the gymnasium, where I made a hiding place in one of the dark corners until the bell rang for my first class.

I was extremely nervous and the thought of running home to change started to plague my desperate mind. There was no way I wanted to be the joke of the entire school on my first day. After moments that felt like eternities, the bell finally rang and it was time to go to class. It was initially hard finding my first few classes, but I managed. I could see that all the other kids were just as confused about the new situation as I was.

I made it on time to every single one of my classes that morning, but the crude jokes followed me into the classroom. I managed to hold back my tears and ignore them. I decided that during lunch I would run the two miles uphill back home and change, then come back as the new cool kid. When the lunch bell finally rang, I took my bag and ran down the hall to the outside where I could push through the back gate and be home free.

As I approached the gate to my freedom, I heard a loud voice say, "Hey, *puto*! You look like Pee Wee Herman, bitch!"

As the terrifying laughter erupted, I stopped dead in my tracks. It was as if I was stuck and sinking in quicksand. Before I had the chance to look behind me, I felt a SMACK! right on my back. As I looked over my left shoulder, the remnants of a peanut butter and jelly sandwich slid down the back of my shirt. I was absolutely horrified. I had just been assaulted by a flying sandwich thrown by a much larger kid laughing and pointing his finger at me. He was dressed like a *cholo* from one of the neighboring projects and I was the object of his most endearing affection. All his friends followed suit, laughing and calling me names in Spanish slang. This sandwich-tosser was obviously the group leader and looked like he weighed a good, hard, lard-heavy 200 pounds. He walked toward me and pushed me onto the floor. I must have flown like a rag doll, because it felt like I had been sacked by Lawrence Taylor. I stood up, knees shaking, scared out of my mind. He pushed me once more right back onto the floor, to show his dominance. He yelled, "Stay there!" I gladly cooperated.

The shame I felt was excruciating. I was feeling that same defeated and horrified sensation that I felt that day at the playground, but getting over this bully would take more than my mother and two sisters. I was once again humiliated and ashamed of myself.

Once he left and I no longer needed permission to stand up, I picked up my sack lunch and decided to go eat it all by myself. I was completely destroyed. I returned to my comfortable hiding spot in the gymnasium bathroom stall, which I decided to make my home for the remainder of the school year. I was too scared to go out there and confront him or face any kind of jokes or laughter at my expense. I'd rather be a coward and save my face and health. This started my new routine of cowering away and running to the gymnasium bathroom every day for lunch.

This went on for most of the first semester. I wasn't able to meet any new friends and my life had turned into an emotional rollercoaster. Every day was the same old drill. I would run out of class right at the bell and get to the familiar bathroom stall to eat my lunch in fear. After about two months of running out of class before the bell could finish its ring, the teacher got curious. He had gotten sick and tired of seeing me run out of class right at the bell, and asked me to stay after class to speak with him. I thought, "Oh no, this man is going to mess up my whole school survival routine!" My eyes widened and I got sick to my stomach. I began sweating profusely and my hands got clammy.

The bell rang and he gestured at me not to move. I sat there and began squirming with anxiety of the future torture I was about to endure. He sat next to me and simply asked why I always ran out of class before the bell could finish ringing. I came up with a generic answer to hopefully satisfy him. It didn't, but I answered all of his questions abruptly and impatiently with nervous lies. After all, I was in a hurry to get the hell out of there so I wouldn't get my ass kicked. He looked at me suspiciously and then let me go on my way, but it was too late.

When I turned out to the hallway to run, I heard that paralyzing voice I was dreading, "Hey, faggot! Where you going, puto?"

I slowly turned around to face him with a nervous smile and gasped, "Nowhere, I'm just gonna head over to eat my lunch."

He sensed my insecurity and started to laugh while walking toward me with a clutched fist. I knew what was coming. My pulse quickened and my knees got unstable. Once he got inside my personal space, he cocked his arm back and punched me square in the chest. He hit me so hard I dropped my lunch. The sound of it echoed throughout the hallway. I let out a loud gasp as the air escaped my lungs. Holding back tears, I bent down to pick up my lunch and felt the sensation of warm urine spilling out all over the crotch of my jeans. I looked down in horror and saw that I was pissing myself. My tormentor burst out laughing. I was horrified.

I turned back around and walked as fast as I could back to my familiar hiding place, the bathroom stall, my sanctuary of cowardly misfortune. It felt like the entire school was laughing at me. There really was no place to run and hide anymore. I was forever ruined. My reputation would forever be known as the kid who pissed his pants at school. Then I heard an unfamiliar voice speak out and say, "Hey, man. Leave that dude alone, bro! That's not fuckin' cool!" I looked back and saw Danny, who would later become one of my life-long best friends. He followed me to the restroom while speaking in Spanish to the bullies behind me. He walked into the restroom with me and patted me on the back in consolation while handing me paper towels to wipe myself clean. I was literally covered in piss and tears.

We talked in the bathroom for the rest of the lunch period and he watched me break down uncontrollably. The fourth period bell was about to ring when he said, "Hey, bro, you wanna just ditch class and get the fuck out of here?"

I looked up at him in despair and, seeing no other options and being too humiliated to face the school, I nodded and said, "Let's get the fuck outta here, man. Screw this hellhole." This was the beginning of an awesome, but troubling, friendship.

CHAPTER 6

BREAKING MY PARENTS' HEARTS

What started as innocent jokes in the classroom soon escalated. I wanted to get my adrenaline fix by messing with the law. I knew I wasn't going to continue going to school anymore anyway, so why not find stimulation elsewhere? Every day I would show up to school, meet Danny and a few other misfits, and bolt by the second period. That gave us just enough time to get things coordinated. We would all meet in the restroom in B Hall and wait patiently for about fifteen minutes for security to finish their routine drills. We already knew their patterns. They had the same routine over and over. Once we got by security, we would climb up and over the ten-foot-high chain-link fence and run our little asses off to freedom.

We would take the underground tunnels that zigged and zagged under most of the west side of El Paso and explore the inner city from the viewpoint of the rats and sewage, with only the light from our pocket lighters to shield us from the darkness. It was actually a cool experience. We had the chance to meet a few homeless people that called the tunnel system their home. I loved speaking with them and listening to their fascinating life stories. I was always the one asking the deep personal questions and investigating for further information.

Once we made our way through most of the tunnel system, there was an intersection where the tunnel met the sewer line. We hid our stash of weed and playboys in that juncture and spent our days ditching school, smoking weed, and staring at tits, surrounded by human crap. I still don't understand how we thought that was even remotely acceptable. After wasting a few hours doing that, we would head to Danny's house and hang out some more, watching porn on his dad's big screen television. Whatever was on the menu for that day, we did. There was usually some form of vandalism, shoplifting, and then hiding out from police in the underground tunnel system.

Obviously my parents started to notice that I never had any homework, as well as the sudden change in my attitude and style. I was starting to rebel against everything that had anything to do with authority, including my parents. I didn't want any lecture from either of them. They didn't need to know their son felt like a coward and was scared to go to school. I was dealt this hand and I was going to play it the way I saw fit.

After a few weeks of this chronic absenteeism, the teachers started calling my house. Sometimes I was lucky enough to answer the telephone and disguise my voice as my mother's. I hadn't hit puberty yet, so the teachers fell for my concerned, conflicted, and sorrowful voice every time. I would pretend to cry on the phone and weep in painful disappointment over my imaginary son. I'd frequently have to put the phone on mute so I could burst out laughing as the teacher or principal fell for my line of horse shit. Many times they didn't seem to know how to react, so they would say how sorry they were and put someone else from the office in rotation for the next call.

I ended up getting very creative with this process, I would

sometimes pretend that they had called while I was having sex. I would breathe like I was hyperventilating and yell out vulgar Spanish words and phrases. My favorite was, "*Aye papi metalo a su culo, cabron!*" I'd take a second to listen to the response. They knew my mother was white, so I'm pretty sure they were confused on the issue and thought my father was cheating. Usually they were so embarrassed that they would just immediately hang up the phone. This was hilarious to me, but I was smooth sailing down the drain of complete and utter failure. I was outsmarting the whole school and police system while loving every second of the process. I even went to the Kinko's printing shop and faked my report card. I was an outstanding A and B student to my parents. I threw a C or D in there from time to time to make it more realistic and to lower any suspicion. We didn't have internet back then, so grades weren't available online like they are now. My next graduation was staying out late with the guys and causing all kinds of trouble at night. This act of rebellion really started to worry my parents. They would stay up late every night worrying about what time I would return home. What I did to those two was absolutely unforgivable. I would take it all back today if I could.

One of my favorite deviant behaviors started when I discovered where my dad would lay his keys at night. Like a ninja, I'd crawl quietly on my hands and knees into their room at 2 A.M., while making sure any loud movements I made were timed in sync with my father's snoring. I would sneak back out of my parents' room, keys in hand, then sneak out the front door to roll the car down the street a bit so I could start it without the dogs barking, waking up the neighbors and my parents. I didn't even know how to drive, so I had to learn by doing. I would run and jump into the car while it was rolling down the hill and switch on the ignition. I would press the gas until I could feel it become an extension of me. I hauled ass down the hill in record time each night to pick up all my buddies, who were quietly waiting on the corner outside the gas station.

Once I picked them up, we would laugh all the way to El Paso's sister city, Juárez, Mexico, where we cut our teeth on the art of hustling, partying, and crime. We would cross over the filth-ridden, congested Mexican-American Bridge, fake IDs in hand, and party with the much older high school kids. It was pre-9/11, so everyone at customs was lenient. It was basically a joke. They just saw kids having fun and didn't tamper with the natural process. Our nights usually began with all of us taking tequila shots, then drowning ourselves with beer and vodka, followed by the ritual of puking it all out by 5 A.M.

This went on three times a week, at least. It didn't matter how many times my parents caught me sneaking into their room, nothing stopped me from getting the keys and going to Mexico. I would try again until I succeeded. Every night I was successful and we would run for the Mexican border. Mexico made us feel like we were true outlaws. We would drink, party, engulf ourselves in women and hookers. We would hang out in the streets all night and even place bets on the local dog races or bull fights. We could get in all sorts of trouble and basically hand a cop twenty to fifty dollars to buy our way out of it. If any of us got arrested, even buying the cop a hooker for the night would get us out of a jam. Juárez territory became familiar and I knew all the club owners and bartenders by name at the age of thirteen.

Most times after we crossed back over to the El Paso side, we would go to some fast food joint like Whataburger, order cheeseburgers with cartons of fries, and stuff our drunk faces until we were content. Once I dropped everyone back off, I would rush home and be in bed by 5 A.M., when everything went as planned. Most times they did, but my fail-safe plan wasn't always fail-safe. There were a few times my plan didn't work out. Every now and then I'd return home to find my parents nervously waiting for me to come home safely. They would usually report the car stolen and have the police send out a search for me. The worst times were when I would return home drunk to a welcoming party of cops inside the house. They would arrest me on the spot for theft of a motor vehicle and underage intoxication. Before long it was my parents that were getting in trouble for my reckless behavior.

This crazy merry-go-round lasted a full year until I saw my mother finally break down into tears. It broke my heart to see my mother like that. I couldn't do that to the people I loved anymore. I had to straighten my act up. I loved my mother and father and I could tell that I was crucifying them. Getting arrested every other week wasn't funny anymore. It was a level of criminal insanity that needed to stop before I hurt myself or innocent bystanders, or any of my loved ones. I needed to make a severe change and deal with my demons.

I went back to school and dealt with the torment of being bullied. So what if I got my ass kicked a few times, at least I wouldn't break my parents' hearts anymore. It wasn't so bad once I went back to school and got used to it. I just blocked out the cruel jokes and nasty comments. My grades still weren't the best, but I managed to pass by the skin of my teeth. Maybe the teachers felt sympathy for me because they knew my situation and saw me really put forth an effort. I'll never know.

As the school year ended and summer came and went once more, I started trying to make new friends, but they were just no fun. My former friends were a crazy cast of characters. There was never a dull moment with those guys. These new friends were boring, complete squares. It was agony hanging out with them. The highlight of their day was a good game of Nintendo.

I went into eighth grade with every intention to stick it out and pass, but I just couldn't resist trouble. It followed me like a shadow. I went to four different schools that year and was mainly in alternative programs. I didn't understand how to behave in class and I was acting out due to my insecure feelings from being the target of school bullies. It was too much to face, so getting in trouble was my primary occupation. My mother would go to school, pleading and begging for them not to expel her son; if they could only see where this problem really stemmed from, they would take a more sympathetic approach, she would tell them.

After this broken record, the only thing left were the "special" classes in a school that was out of my district. It was Lincoln Junior High, and Paul Strelzin was the principal. He was one of the funniest, most charismatic, and loudest principals anywhere on earth. He was an old friend of the family and decided to take the David Rodriguez project head on. He allowed me to go to Lincoln, but he made me enroll in B.I.C., Behavioral Improvement Class. I didn't think this was going to be so bad, until the next morning when the bus pulled up in front of my house and honked for me to come outside. This wasn't just some ordinary school bus, it was the short kind, the one with kids in helmets, licking the windows. As if I couldn't get any more embarrassed, I was on a bus with kids wearing diapers and screaming vulgar language, drooling uncontrollably. The ride to school was a long, humiliating, and agonizing journey across town. Once we approached the school I would hide a notebook over my face when I got off, just like on the Court TV programs when someone didn't want to get seen or recognized.

My first day in B.I.C. was the most shocking. I took a seat next to a kid named George. George looked over and decided to explain the rules of engagement to me while making the most foul, hilarious faces. "You're gonna love it here, watch this shit," he said, then he stood up, yelled "Fuck you" at the teacher, and threw his desk through the chalk board. All the other kids began to laugh and mimic the sounds of monkeys. I couldn't believe that shit. All George got was a timeout and a trip to the corner of the room, which he proceeded to piss all over.

Miss Austin, a nice, heavy-set black lady, stood up, pointing, and yelled out, "Ahhhhhh hell, no, George! You crazy boy! What the hell is wrong witchu? Yo momma drop you as a baby or something?"

Then the other kids would erupt in laughter. This was the show that was put on for the rest of the day. Sometimes George would be sent for a trip to see our class counselor to listen to his problems. He returned with an apology to Miss Austin and a huge smirk. I immediately felt at home and I knew right then that this was going to be gravy. It wasn't before the end of the period that I could no longer resist joining the party. I was making monkey sounds and jack off gestures to the teacher while cracking jokes at her expense.

After weeks of this animalistic behavior, I realized what a sweet lady Miss Austen really was. I think she saw that bad kids deep down wanted to be good, because sometimes she would take me aside to say, "David, I know you're smarter than this and come from a good family. You'll figure yourself out and get sharp. These classes aren't for you, you're better than this." She knew exactly how to tug on my heart strings and defuse my troublemaking patterns. I was sick and tired of letting people down and hurting the people that loved and believed in me. I started to feel extremely guilty. I knew that I needed to stop my redundant bullshit and to help Miss Austen help me.

After the fifth week of school hell, I started to straighten up and really try to get back into regular classes. I needed to get reintegrated into regular society before I grew up like some weird whack job with a matching set of antisocial personality issues. This wasn't for me anymore and I was acting the fool. I decided to focus on my grades and put an effort into my studies for the first time. I passed the eighth grade and made my parents, Paul Streltzin and Miss Austin proud. Miss Austin said that she'd better not see me in that class again. I figured that was the least I could give her for being so kind and understanding.

As the school year ended and summer came, the school turbulence had petered out, but more trouble was brewing on the horizon.

CHAPTER 7

DIVINE INTERVENTION, OR A CHANCE ENCOUNTER

Joe Sullivan with his son Bear

Joe Sullivan with coach Rocky Galarza after Golden Gloves win

I t was the first week of summer and my dad knew trouble was ahead. Late nights, arrests, and partying kept appearing on the horizon. He decided to take a last chance Hail Mary and throw me into something that might stick. He asked me to go on a ride along with him, to talk about my concerns and troubles. We ended up in the parking lot of the San Juan Recreation Center and Boxing Gym. I couldn't believe it—our nice, little father-son bonding moment was held under false pretenses, albeit with good intentions.

The San Juan Recreation Center and Boxing Gym was a community center where many of the old boxing professionals would pass through to train. It saw such greats such as Julio César Chávez and Randall "Tex" Cobb. It even was visited by the great Muhammad Ali. It was a historic landmark of El Paso. There was the distinct smell of dingy leather when we walked into the gym. This smell came to mean home, for a time. The blare of AC/DC's "Hell's Bells" was pulsing through the air. We heard the loud ring from the boxing bell signaling that it was work time. I'll never forget watching the kids beat the bags to the rhythm of the music. They had an energy to them I'd already long forgotten.

My dad called the head trainer over and said, "You wanna see something special? Give this kid the gloves and put him on a bag." The trainer looked at my father with a humorous look and kindly obliged. He brought the gloves and sat them next to me.

I stared at them before I looked up at my dad and asked, "Why?"

Before I could say no, the trainer was signaling me to come over to him so he could lace up my gloves. I decided that give it an honest try, for his sake only. As I started to warm up, a strange sensation came over me. I started to feel incredibly strong and fast. It was like I hadn't missed a beat from childhood. I gained some confidence and began shadowboxing to show off my rapid hand speed to the other kids. I did a few rounds and had the feeling of all eyes fixated on me. I had the unique feeling of being the object of envy and significance. It was a foreign and alien feeling of acceptance. I decided to walk over to the bag and crank up all cylinders to demonstrate my power and speed with full force. The rafters started to shake every time I landed a good combination on the bag. I knew I looked like a phenomenon. The gym stared at me in silence as I ended my workout. I punched like a powerful grown man at the age of fourteen. My dad just sat back in his chair with a proud grin.

As I took the gloves off, sweating and catching my breath, I saw a mountain of a man approaching my dad. He was my dad's height, but younger, and had a huge Jay Leno jaw. I saw him introduce himself to my father and pull him aside to speak with him. I knew I recognized his face, but I couldn't place where. A few moments quickly passed and they both approached me.

The big, square-jawed man said, "Hey, Kid, I'm Officer Joe Sullivan. I've picked you up on calls a few times. What I just witnessed, I've never seen by a kid your age before. Why aren't you taking the sport of boxing seriously?"

I didn't know how to answer, so I just shrugged my shoulders at him. He glanced back over at my dad and told him that he would pick me up from school every day and take me to the boxing gym if I stopped getting into trouble at school and with the police. He said that he couldn't just stand back and watch me waste my God-given talent.

I didn't know how to respond except to say, "Sure, okay, that's a deal." But in the back of my mind I knew there was no way this dude actually cared that much. I doubted that he was going to drive all the way to my school every day just to pick me up and then take me to the boxing gym all the way across town. I called his bluff.

When the first day of school started and the last bell rang for the day, I walked out to see a huge silhouette of a police officer leaning against his cruiser, aviator sunglasses with a Jay Leno jaw.

I was wrong about Officer Sullivan. He was serious about his promise. He was there every day after school, leaning against the cop car. He never missed a day. He would give me a high-five as I walked out from my last class, put me in the front seat of his vehicle and drive me off to the San Juan Boxing Gym so we could both train.

Riding in a cop car without handcuffs was a new experience for me, and I appreciated the positive attention. I could only imagine what my peers thought. The year before I was riding the short bus to school, and the next year I'm riding shotgun in a police car to a boxing gym. I could feel the kids watch me in confusion as I slid into the front seat of the police vehicle. Maybe they just thought I was that dangerous and needed to be escorted out of school by a personal guard. Suddenly, and for the first time ever, I felt cool. I owe so much to Joe Sullivan. He was the big brother I never had but badly needed. After weeks of going to San Juan Boxing gym, we figured it was time for a change and a new atmosphere. San Juan was always closed for some obscure holiday and opened late on the weekends. The monthly fees were annoying as well. They'd hassle you over five dollars a month. After getting sick of this, we made our move. We decided to give Rocky's Bar and Gym a try. Yes, you read that correctly, Rocky's Bar and Gym.

CHAPTER 7½

MY BRIGHT IDEA

I t was the early 1990s and "Yo! MTV Raps" was live and on the air, playing videos of the fresh new faces on the scene. These were the likes of Public Enemy, Dr. Dre, Too Short, and MC Hammer. Gangsta rap and hip-hop were just starting to trickle into the culture. This was the first real mainstream wave to overtake rock and heavy metal, carrying legitimately new and creative voices into the social consciousness. The grunge group, Nirvana, had made a contribution to the airwaves with a huge hit. Everyone was full of "Teen Spirit." It was a momentous time in music history. Two genres occupied the mainstream of music. Barriers were broken down and music was making a shift. The 1990s will forever belong to gangsta rap, hip-hop, and grunge for the suburban white kids of the time. Everyone was either a grunge kid or a gangsta. Gangsta rap was on the top of the charts for most of the high-testosterone, post-puberty kids. Hormones were raging and everyone wanted to be some kind of tough ass. They wanted to represent their hood and be the tough guys, even in an upper-class suburb. All I knew is that I wanted in and at any price.

One day, Danny and I saw the movie *Blood In Blood Out*, which was also called *Bound By Honor*. It was a Latino street gang movie about living in the barrio. It was set and mainly filmed in East LA, but every kid in El Paso identified with it. You needed to be a gangsta if you were gonna be anybody in this world. Shit, I knew of middle-class kids that were being constantly thrown into juvenile hall, all because they wanted to be gangsta. They wanted to prove that they had some kind of real street cred. I went to school and watched the gangstas from the projects lean against the cafeteria wall during lunch time, making obnoxious whistling sounds at the girls that walked by. They'd be wearing the baggy Dickies jeans, suspenders, white wife-beater tank tops, and the black, lace-up Cortez shoes. I thought it was the coolest display I had ever seen. These guys all looked so mature, each one had scruff or a mustache. I was still trying to grow hair on my balls. I realize now that it was because they were held back year after year and some were eighteen years old. In my school, these were like the guys everyone listened to in the prison yard while they made the white boys their little punk bitches. There were a few black kids at our school, and they formed their own little cliques as well. If you went to any of the keg parties and both these groups were there, you'd better leave quickly because it was about to get really ugly. It wasn't rare that fights would break out at the parties and you'd hear gunshots. The most dangerous kids were the posers trying to prove themselves.

As Danny and I exited the movie, my mind birthed the most brilliant and ridiculous idea. I walked out of that movie proud of my Mexican heritage and inspired to be a gangsta. I shadowboxed with Danny as we walked away from the theater shouting Spanish jokes at each other about our mothers.

We constantly did that shit to each other. I guess it was a sign of affection.

Then, like lightning, an idea struck me and left me standing there, silenced. After a few moments of silent inspiration, I said, "Danny! Dude! I figured it out, bro!"

He laughed at me and said, "What, bro?"

I said, "We need to join a gang for our protection, bro!"

"You understand you gotta be jumped in, right?"

I just said, "We gotta be men, bro. We gotta man up for once and be hard!"

I couldn't believe how easily persuaded he was. After discussing the pros and cons, we came to an agreement and decided to go prospecting for gangs the very next day, as if we were looking for a new house or brand new car. We had no idea what we were doing and it was going to be painfully obvious to us by the end of the experience that we had unwittingly and officially become posers.

The next day I went around school talking to the five main gang leaders. There was Jackie's, Machuka, Latin Crips, Sandoval, and the Young Niggas. The last one I was automatically excluded from for obvious reasons. The other four gangs all seemed good, but different gangs wanted different things that would benefit them. You could join as an honorary member with any of them, as long as you provided something of value to them in return. That meant if you paid the rich white kid club membership, you wouldn't have to get jumped in. Not me, though. I wanted the full experience and I wanted to be gang legit. I wanted to come into the gang as a hardass, fully respected. I even had my gang name picked out. I wanted to be the White Rooster, in memory of my dead bird.

I introduced Danny to them and we all discussed where

the initiation would take place. They gave us no time to prepare. "Today, after school, at the baseball field."

Danny and I looked at each other and gasped, "*Orale* bro, *simon que si*," which means, in slang Spanish, "Right on, let's do it."

I went back to the rest of my classes and stared down the clock, ticking ever so slowly. Every period lasted an eternity while I counted down the minutes and seconds. I was nervous and scared out of my mind. I raised my hand to go to the restroom at least eight times during the rest of the day, where I would practice my moves for my big graduation into gangland. I even saw Danny in the restroom one of the times and I said to him, "You nervous, bro?" He responded by running to the toilet and puking uncontrollably. I took that as a resounding yes.

We both knew we couldn't get out of it at this point and it was already less than two periods away. I made him put his hands up in the bathroom so I could show him some basic boxing moves. He was a black belt in tae kwon do, and wanted to rely on his flying kick bullshit. I tried to show him how to bend at the body and cover up once they all started getting their shots in, so we wouldn't risk damage to the organs. My inspired, macho idea after seeing that ridiculous movie was starting to feel like the worst decision I had ever made.

When the final bell rang, Danny and I met by the lockers and pumped each other up with false confidence. We butted heads and gave each other high-fives until our hands and heads were red. As we walked out of the locker area heading to the baseball field, we noticed the whole school following us. They had found out and decided to provide our ass-kicking with an audience. It occurs to me now that this experience was officially the first time I ever performed in front of a crowd.

We walked briskly up to the park and noticed all of the cars parked in a circle around the baseball field. It reminded me of the video game Street Fighter. The vibrations and rattling of the bass bumping in all the cars set the scene for the whole school to see a show, a real live gang initiation at its finest. They would actually witness two poser white boys get jumped into the Machuka gang and enjoy every last second of it. We walked up to our new-found family, having decided that we would not try to fight together because that would only bring them all together in a smaller area. That would benefit them in providing us with more of a beating. We decided to space out about twenty feet apart so that the gang would have to split up, limiting the amount of hits each of us would have to take. Within seconds of our arrival, they put their drinks down and started punching each other on the shoulders, then started jumping up and down. It was definitely going to happen.

As Danny and I started backing up, the punches started flying, the crowd roaring every time they connected. I threw a couple punches here and there, but I had to cover up because too many punches were coming at me too fast and too hard. I had at least ten members of my future family punching and kicking me. I felt the knuckles slice my skin and saw bright fireworks each time I felt a kid's gold ring gash my eye. All I knew at that point was that I had to tuck my chin down and cover up. They kept asking me if I wanted to give up. Those are words you don't say yes to unless you want to get your ass kicked even harder, and then you're not allowed in the gang. You'd have to go to school and endure beatings for the rest of the school year. At least, that's what my research had told me.

I kept saying "No! Keep it coming!"

I would occasionally glance at Danny and see how he

was holding up. He had finally taken my initial advice and was covering up for dear life.

With no ending in sight, I saw that these guys were just starting to have fun and had no intention of stopping. I panicked. Danny was screaming at me, "This was your bright idea, you asshole!"

Both of our faces were a bloody mess and the punches still kept blasting us. It seemed like the mollywhop lasted an eternity. That ass-beating made tag team WWE Wrestling look like child's play. The better part of fifteen minutes, by a conservative estimate, had passed when the most beautiful, angelic sound I'd ever heard approached from the distance. It was police sirens. I knew our beating would be over. The gang scattered and the sounds of rubber tires peeling against the parking lot asphalt faded away from the sirens. The cops sprinted over to both of us and yelled for us to both freeze and put our hands behind our heads. We couldn't have run if we tried. We'd been beaten beyond recognition.

As the cops approached to cuff us, one of them looked at my bloody face and said, "I got this one. I'm gonna question him." I glanced up and recognized Joe Sullivan. I said, "Am I going to jail?" He hushed me and shook his head, no. He did say that I needed to get my butt to the nearest hospital, immediately. He radioed his partners and told them I needed stitches and medical attention. He loosely handcuffed me and put me in the back of the police car. I was dripping blood all over the plastic seating. He drove, lecturing me all the way, to Providence Hospital where I received a new set of twenty stitches with a handful of C-scans to measure internal damage. Then, after a few hours, I was cleared and he brought me back home.

Danny didn't get off as lucky. They threw his ass in jail, and after they spent hours questioning him, he finally came clean and told them it was my bright idea after watching that stupid movie. We became the laughingstock of the entire police force. I couldn't do anything right. I couldn't even get jumped into a gang correctly. To this day, that story is told among old high school friends amid waves of laughter.

CHAPTER 7¾

MUGGED INTO MANHOOD

M y high school class had the biggest desert bonfire parties; they could be seen for miles. We literally had a third-world desert country at our disposal any time we wanted to break away. It was just a skip and a hop over the bridge to Mexico, across the muddy, stagnated and partially dried excuse for a river we called, ironically, the Rio Grande. During the murder season, a person could see a bloated body, floating in the river or washed up on the bank, tangled in weeds. Juárez used to be the most exciting party town in the Southwest, until it became the murder capital of the world. It had the misfortune of hosting the serial killings of women in the thousands, mass grave sites, and regular shootings, sometimes involving kids. It became a place of evil, but my generation was lucky enough to experience it at its peak. We soaked up the last great remnants of old Mexico and lived like outlaws.

We took full advantage of living on the border. It was something no other kid in the nation could understand, except those crossing over to Tijuana or Laredo. In a lot of ways, it was still the Wild West. It was pre-9/11, so it lacked our modern-day propaganda and paranoia. People were in generally good spirits and they were making and spending money like crazy. The economy was going strong. Crossing the border to Juárez, we found our freedom from the reality of our adolescent problems, like living with our parents, school, and the daily regimen. It was a place a kid could go to act like an adult who breaks off to Vegas for some good fun. It was a five-minute walk to freedom, just by crossing the border. Once we crossed, we could gamble on dog races, cock fights, and bull fights, or hit any club we wanted; but the best times were when American high school students were throwing a big party.

Printed flyers would cover high school parking lots across El Paso, letting the kids know which club was going to be the happening place that weekend. Just about every bar on the strip had "five dollar drink and drown." That meant you paid five bucks and got unlimited drinks and tequila shots all night long. I never understood how they made money at this, until I saw that they watered down the alcohol behind closed doors.

We would park our cars on the American side, by the bridge, and take the brisk walk over to the Mexican side. We'd feel the bone-chilling wind, with the bass blasting from the cars that chose to drive over, trunks rattling and shaking like our teeth. I can still smell the familiar odor of backed-up sewage in the streets, the smell of street tacos cooking, and the potent bathroom cleaner that they always used in the bar restrooms. I always crossed the bridge with a huge knot in my stomach, never knowing what would happen on any given night.

One particular night shaped my perspective and altered my worldview forever. It was a Sunday night and a whole group of us wanted to knock back some cold Mexican beers while maybe listening to some mariachis. We liked to regroup on Sundays after the insane weekend, with the late-night parties and troublemaking. We used to meet at the Kentucky Club, which was a well-known bar located just a couple of blocks from the brightly lit-up strip. There, we could play music from the jukebox or tip the Mariachis a measly twenty dollars to play music for us for a good hour.

The Kentucky Club has been a popular establishment in Juárez since the early 1900s, and maybe as far back as the 1800s. It still had its original antique bar, hand-crafted out of solid oak with precise and artistic detailing. Along the thirty-foot bar was a gutter at the floor. This gutter was actually used as a pissing urinal in the old days. The Mexican rancheros and the cowboys from the American side would go to this little hideout in old Mexico, get some cheap entertainment and then be too drunk to stumble to the restroom. It was easier to keep a place at the bar by standing up and urinating on the spot. Obviously when I was patronizing the establishment they wouldn't allow people to do that, and if they caught someone trying to urinate at the bar, they'd have them arrested for indecent exposure before kicking the living shit out of them. Being the punk kid that I was, I got away with it many times. I'd order a big group of drinks to distract the bartender, then proceed to relieve myself into the gutter. If the old outlaws could do it, then so could David Rodriguez. In my mind, I was no different and I had to mark my territory every time I visited. I so badly wanted to emulate and do as the old outlaws did.

That Sunday evening, we were hammering back some cold beers and counting out the money that we had made from the parties we threw that weekend. The Kentucky Club was alive with Mariachi music and the atmosphere was glowing with young faces, tasty food, and limitless alcohol. I began catching a buzz and decided that I'd had enough for the evening. I wanted to collect my portion of the money and start walking back over the bridge to get home. My portion was $1500 and I was exhausted. The only desire I had was to get home, stash my money under the mattress and get some sleep for the long week of training and school. I shook all my buddies' hands good-bye and hugged Danny and Matthew before I pushed my way out the door. I put the fat roll of money down my front jean pocket and began the short walk back over the bridge.

As I walked, I remembered that the dog races were in just a few days. I couldn't resist making a slight detour to the sports book to make a bet. As I walked down the strip, I pulled out my cash and carelessly counted out five hundred dollars. As I approached the sports book I noticed the sound of footsteps behind me. The footsteps got louder as their pace quickened. Fear started to consume me and adrenaline overtook my body. I decided to quicken my pace as well. I picked up to a half-jog. I didn't want to look scared or ridiculous, but my instincts were telling me to rush my pace. I could see the front entrance and the doors were getting closer. I heard a BAM BAM like two fire-crackers going off next to my eardrums. I knew those sounds were not firecrackers and I was in serious trouble. My quick paced jog now turned into a full-on sprint with the sounds of footsteps behind me. I decided to make a right turn into a dark back alley and try looping around back to the bridge. My heart was pounding through my chest and I was running for my life. I was jumping over fire hydrants and dodging oncoming cars, but I could still hear them behind me. I ran and tears flowed down my cheeks as I prayed out loud for God to save me.

Then the unthinkable happened. I ran into a dead end. Nothing but a wall separated my freedom from gunfire. I ran up the wall like a desperate dog, but couldn't scale it. I was trapped. As I pressed against the wall, my back against the cold concrete, I saw two thugs turn the corner, their guns still pointed at me. They started to approach me slowly while speaking Spanish. I couldn't understand them and I knew my life was about to end. I closed my eyes and cried helplessly. As I stood there I felt a cold barrel against the side of my dome. They both started frantically searching my pockets, and found the desired wad of cash. They began counting the money out loud, right in front of me. I resumed praying for my life. This had to be it.

Mid-prayer, two police sirens blurted out. I opened one eye to see what was going on. Two Mexican cop cars blocked the only way out. The thugs started screaming and yelling at the cops in Spanish. I was standing, frozen and afraid, not daring to make a sound. I couldn't move a muscle. The thugs started to move to my right side, not thinking to take me as a hostage. The cops were barricaded behind the front side doors of their vehicles with their guns drawn. An exchange of fire echoed throughout the alley. The thugs dropped to the ground and my cash fell along with them. The money began to blow in the wind, intermingling with the trash in the alley. The cops holstered their firearms and scraped up all the money their pockets could fit. I watched in horror as the police officers robbed two lifeless bodies lying twenty feet from me. I gently slid down the wall and onto the floor and lay still. As I heard the slight wind whistling through the trash cans and empty garbage lids, I heard the police jump back into their cars and slowly pull away.

Shortly afterwards, I picked myself up and dusted off my jeans, making my way out of the dark alley. As I walked, I heard one of the thugs gasping for air and making grunting noises. I decided to walk over to him. As I approached my eyes widened at the horror I witnessed. His chest was completely blown out and blood was pooling around his entire body. We locked eyes for a few moments. I stood paralyzed as I watched him take his last few gasps of air and then surrender his life to the unknown.

I began backing out of the alley as my mind tried to process what just had happened. People flooded into the alley after hearing the gun shots. They were as horrified as I was, except I could hear nothing. My senses became detached and numb as I walked away. I noticed the looks of curiosity and disgust. I felt random hands reaching and tugging on my torn shirt as I started to make my way through the crowd of onlookers. In the distance I heard the sounds of ambulances and police cars. Then a realization hit me. I'm not in America. I just witnessed a homicide and robbery by crooked police officers. They're going to want to question me and that means they would detain me for the night and possibly even kill me.

My street instincts kicked into overdrive and I pushed the person who was trying to console and contain me for the police. I pushed him with the force of a middle linebacker. I knew he had good intentions, but I was in fear for my life. I sprinted full speed toward the border as I had done many times, but with a newfound panic. I was knocking down pedestrians and running through traffic. As I approached the border bridge, I saw a cop car patrolling with a spot light. I hoped to hell they didn't see me. I stopped dead in my tracks and made a quick left into a gordita taco shop.

I walked in, out of breath, and the owner just looked at me, puzzled. I decided it was best not to look panicked or guilty, so I cracked a smile and pointed at my fists and knuckles. I told him, "*Pinche chingasos en pinche discoteque!*" He started to laugh with me and then asked what I wanted to eat. I ordered a chicken torta and took a seat at the plastic table. I patiently watched as the cop car crept down the street shining its spot light onto anything it thought could be suspicious. They rolled slowly past my position and looked right at me. They saw me calmly sitting, waiting for my food. I was holding my breath, beads of sweat trickling down the sides of my temples. They stopped for a second and my stomach dropped. I thought fast and just reacted. I smiled while giving them a thumbs up and a nod. They looked puzzled, but they nodded back at me and pressed the gas. I was home free. I outwitted the whole situation.

I decided not to run back, but to play the rest of my journey calmly so that I wouldn't bring attention to myself. I paid for my torta and made my way out the door. Luckily the thugs left me with the pesos in my back pocket. I had just enough for the torta and the bridge crossing. As soon as I crossed over to the American side, I fell to my knees and kissed the ground. I was never so proud to be alive and to be an American citizen. *Ahhh thank you, God! Ahhhh thank you, God! Lord, thank you for having mercy on me!!* I kept repeating this mantra over and over out loud as I kissed the filthy ground.

There are moments in life when everything you know gets turned upside down. You never know from one minute to the next when your life may be in jeopardy. I thought I was a dead man that night, but for some crazy reason someone upstairs decided to smile upon me. I didn't know what my future would hold, but I knew my guardian angels were definitely going to work overtime. It would prove to be one hell of a task.

CHAPTER 8

ROCKY

Rocky's bar and gym was hidden under a bridge overpass in the 'hood of Alberta Street, on the east side of El Paso. There were heavy sounds of highway traffic mixed with the occasional blare of the Santa Fe train pushing through the neighborhood every couple of hours. All around that area was low-income housing and Rocky's Bar was the local watering hole.

As Officer Joe Sullivan and I rolled up to Rocky's Bar, we could hear the loud thumping Tejano music blasting from the inside of the bar. As we pulled up to the front, we saw the bar doors fly open with two heavy Mexican bouncers and Rocky Galarza himself struggling to throw out an uncooperative, drunk and belligerent customer. My first impression of Rocky communicated his temper loud and clear. He kept cursing at the man in Spanish while pulling and pushing him onto the street. The guy tripped and fell like a wet rag doll, hitting his head on the hard pavement. Rocky wasn't done there. He had to make sure that the tip of his cowboy boot found a suitable place on the man's jaw. He ran over and kicked the man's head in like it was fourth down and punt. He almost launched the poor bastard headfirst. The man's teeth sprayed all over the street like broken Christmas tree ornaments.

Rocky looked out of breath. He glanced up at us and asked in a rough voice, "How may I be of service to you fellas?"

Joe and I looked in disbelief at each other and I took the initiative to respond. "We are here to check out your gym and hopefully get a workout in, sir."

He chuckled and replied, "Well, this is a real gym, I train real fighters. This isn't a place to just get your workout in. You can do that in your mama's garage." My understanding of this man's character deepened. I believed that he had to be missing a few screws upstairs and I wanted no part of his crazy machismo. I thought, *I'll just work out here one day and then get back to the old routine at San Juan boxing gym tomorrow. Screw this crazy-tempered wild man.*

As these hesitant thoughts drifted through my mind, I saw him waving at us to come around the back, where the gym was located. We walked to the back and set our gym bags down, then we watched as he went over to the side and dialed his cordless phone. After a few moments of wondering why he looked so frantic, I started to eavesdrop. It sounded like severe and serious business. It was mostly in Spanish, so I couldn't make out much of it. He slammed the phone down, clapped his hands together and yelled out over to us, "Let's see what kind of girls we got in here today!" I couldn't ignore the strange eagerness in the pit of my stomach.

Joe and I went ahead and wrapped up our hands and started to warm up. The gym was located outside in the back of the bar, so there was a slight wind pushing sand into our eyes, along with the baking heat from the desert sun. After a few rounds had passed with Joe and I going through our routine shadowboxing exhibition, Rocky came back outside from the bar with three rough and mean-looking youngsters. They had shaved heads, gang tattoos and blank, lifeless stares. They came into the gym clearly wanting to kick somebody's ass. They glanced over at me with a hateful stare. They sat down and began wrapping their hands while speaking in a broken Spanish slang I couldn't understand. I got a queasy and uneasy feeling inside my gut. I knew something had to be up. Rocky walked over and studied me with his experienced eyes. I could tell he was looking at my shadowboxing movements and calculating the instructions he would have to give to his fighters. I was being studied for destruction and it made me uneasy.

Then Rocky leaned against one of the heavy bags with his elbows and began a conversation with me. "How you feelin'?"

"Umm, I dunno, I guess good?"

Rocky looked at me with disgust. "You're not sure how you feel? Do you need to ask your mother or something? You got some kind of little girlfriend fucking with your feelings? I'm going to ask you again, how do you feel?"

I stopped shadowboxing and looked at him uncertainly, "Okay, I guess good, then?"

"Did you bring your mouthpiece and sparring gear?"

I replied, "No, sir. I've never really sparred before. I just came to hit the bags."

"Well, we don't just hit the bags here. We hit people. Today you're going to fight and if you show me no heart, then you leave my place like a coward immediately. The door is right there." He pointed.

In fear I responded, "Can we do it tomorrow? I honestly don't have my gear, Rocky."

"Honestly? We're about to see you in the most honest place you've ever been. Right here, fighting in the boxing ring.

Today you don't need your gear, I have some for you to use. You brought your pair, right?"

"My pair? What are you saying, sir?"

"YOUR PAIR! YOUR FUCKING BALLS. You brought your balls, right?"

"They were there this morning, sir."

He gave me a fatherly, loving grin and pointed to the ring. "Get in the ring, kid." So, without any further argument, I slowly walked up the steps of the ring and made my way through the ropes, scared out of my mind.

Here was that familiar feeling again, that feeling of petrifying fear. I'd never boxed anybody before. I'd only looked great hitting the bags. *I don't really want to actually do this shit! I just wanna look good and keep in shape and convince people I'm a badass without actually having to prove it!* Except by then it was too late. *I can't look like the coward I am to everyone here. Maybe I'll let him hit me a few times and then I'll find a soft place on the canvas to lay down. Maybe I'll let him hit me to the body one time and take a fall.* All these cowardly thoughts raced through my mind. I wanted so badly to get the fuck out of that man's crazy gym and get back home.

I looked over at Joe, and instead of saying "let's get out of here," he said, "Keep your hands up and throw those punches like you know how, champ!"

This police officer was actually agreeing with this crazy old whack-job of a man? The next thing I knew, Rocky was now gloving me up and putting on my cup. The seconds were moving rapidly and my pulse had quickened. I smiled up at him to show him my teeth.

He said, "What the hell? Why are you smiling at me? You like me or something?"

I said, "No! I need a mouthpiece, man."

He had the audacity to say, "I don't think you'll need it today, just don't get hit." After this he let out a loud chuckle. My impulse was to grab my shit and run out of that gym while screaming, *Fuck you, you crazy old man!* Before I could think any more about my escape, the biggest and meanest of the kids climbed into the ring. He locked eyes with me and started to stretch and shadowbox while waiting for the bell to ring. I knew there was no way out of this situation, so I decided to suck it up and attempt to throw a few punches to see what would happen. I might at least get a sympathetic smile and pat on the back for trying. Then I heard that dreadful sound. The DING DING echoed across the gym and Rocky yelled, "*TIEMPO!* LET'S GO!"

It all happened so fast. The bigger kid came charging right at me, throwing fast, precise punches. I had no idea what to do. For the first part of the round, I just covered up and tried to fend him off. It was of no help. I started to feel overwhelmed and tired. That old familiar feeling of seeing the bright explosion of stars and tasting the iron in my blood rushed back to me. The only difference was this time my lungs were burning and my legs and arms were weak. This was actually hurting me more than when Danny and I got jumped by the gang! He was hitting me in places I couldn't defend. My stomach, then my head, then my arms, then back to my stomach. This kid was a ringer. I would find out later that he had 150 amateur fights and was a real battle-tested, tough little kid. Most of the kids in the barrio by Rocky's gym had at least fifty fights by the time they were fifteen years old. It was almost a part-time hobby of the neighborhood.

As he was kicking my ass, I caught a glimpse of the annoying, shit-eating grin displayed on his face. I didn't like it. I knew he thought I was a joke and I was beginning to realize I couldn't live like this anymore. I owed it to myself to just try and get one good punch. I decided to let one final shot go before I went down. I calculated, launching my left hook. It was the punch I could break bags with. If I can break bags with it, maybe I can buzz him a little and slow his pace down. So I stepped back a bit, took a final breath, zeroed in on his jaw, and stepped right the fuck into it. Then, BOOM! I felt contact. He went down like I had just put a shotgun to his head. There was another BOOM as he hit the canvas.

He laid there motionless. The gym was silent. Rocky was silent. No more crazy comments, just a look of sheer disbelief. Joe stared at the body in amazement. It took Rocky a good five minutes to wake up the disoriented kid and start pouring ice water on his head. The kid had no idea where he was or even what day of the week it was. Rocky handed the ice pitcher over to Joe and commanded him to look over the boy. Then he climbed into the ring with me. He put on his hand pads and started to motion me to punch on them. A stern and serious look overtook his face, and he began to give me direct orders on how to punch and move in the ring. The coaching commenced, and my life changed forever. The only words Rocky said to me that day were, "You're going to be a future champion if you come in here every day and you never quit."

I couldn't believe what he told me. I couldn't believe what I had done. I felt I had been reborn. This brave new me had been hidden inside, but I could never find it. I needed a man like Rocky to help pull it out of me. We all need that guy. We all need a Rocky in our lives, that man that pushes you to that fragile and breakable moment, where you either fold up or you become the person you're destined to be. That day, I found out about the person I was supposed to be. I had been a coward by choice, not by circumstance. I realized in that moment that I possessed the inner power to change it all.

CHAPTER 9

CREATING A MONSTER

Rocky took on the task and began the regimen of training me for countless hours after school. At this point I was a newly licensed driver who was always in a hurry. I would finish my after-school detention and then haul my ass off to the other side of town to begin the schooling of hard knocks. Every day was met head-on with pure excitement, vigor and flourishing love. Rocky and I really started to bond and I began laughing more and more at his rough and witty humor. It began to be a routine for him to take me to Juárez on the weekends to get the proper and necessary sparring for my development. I would spar the best professionals they had to offer, and it became routine for me to knock out one or two of them almost daily. These were mature and grown men. I was a kid of sixteen, knocking out men in their twenties and thirties. The word started to get out about me in the local area and people started to come from all over to watch and bear witness to the rumors of the boy who knocked out men.

After countless weekends sharpening my skills with much more experienced fighters, Rocky decided that it was time for his protégé to take a real amateur fight. In those days amateur fights were a monthly occurrence, and there was going to be an amateur fight in Las Cruces the following month. We used to call the amateur fights, the ones that weren't tournaments, "Smokers." It was a way to get experience and build your resume as a fighter before you registered for the bigger tournaments. I reluctantly agreed to take a fight, and decided to train harder than I ever had before. We began picking up training every day, harder and harder. I would leave the gym hardly able to drive home because I was so unbelievably exhausted.

I was weary, but grateful for such a beautiful and wonderful man to come into my life and mentor me. It wasn't long before he began affectionately calling me "son." I decided to buckle down and focus on boxing much more. Due to my new life as a fighter, it wasn't an option to be out partying and causing havoc. Boxing demanded discipline and there was no room in my life for any other recreational activities.

My confidence as a fighter was beginning to grow and I wasn't taking any shit from anybody. The belief had set in that if I could knock out real fighters, then a wise-ass kid on the street would be no match for me. Within three months of training with Rocky, I decided to settle some scores and knock out three of the infamous kids that had made my life a living hell. I walked up to each one with beaming confidence, said some kind of corny movie line to add to the moment, then socked them square in the mouth. They didn't expect it and they fell, limp, to the ground. The fourth kid that gave me trouble begged for mercy so I decided to have pity, but he still needed to pay. Every day I demanded a payment for my lunch.

I didn't realize it then, but I had become the bully. I believed that this was all personal and it was nothing but proper payback. I was beginning to like the feeling of being feared. I was a sleeping giant awakened. I wanted not just kids but grown men to tremble in fear when I walked into a room. This once-scared little boy had turned into a vicious lion.

When I would lack sparring partners on certain days, Rocky would hold bets with the drunkards inside the bar. He would purposely pick out the large, hot-tempered, masculine men. He would strut up to them and bet their drinking tab that they couldn't beat up the scrawny little sixteen-year-old he had training outside. They would laugh in his face and almost always take the bet. There would be times they wouldn't even make it out to the gym. They would stumble out of the back doors and fall face first onto the cement before ever making it into the ring. Most of the victims he chose were completely incompetent and wasted, but Rocky knew exactly what he was doing. He was feeding his young lion fresh meat and getting him accustomed to the taste of blood. I began feeling a certain strange feeling when he brought them out. I knew I was going to hurt these men, and hurt them badly. It was an addictive power to know I could hurt anybody with my bare hands. It was like giving a heroin junky a hit. Knocking people out became my new fix and I needed the drug badly.

At one point during that week of training, Rocky had fitness camps for all the UTEP football players to come in and stay in shape. He would make the phone call for me to come hurrying over when they began the workout. I would race across town, climb into the ring and just wait for one of them to accept our challenge. They would always laugh and tell Rocky, "I'm not gonna hurt this little kid! He's just a skinny boy!" I would tell them how I fucked their mother last night and then that would be it. They'd jump in the ring, red in the face, pissed off and ready to behead me.

"Okay, you little shit. You asked for it."

I would laugh in their face and tell their friends, "Better take a picture of me standing over him when he's knocked out on the floor."

They would always laugh and then, moments later, the laughing would turn into moans and groans as they watched their star linebacker or tight end begin to get completely annihilated. After about twenty seconds to a minute of us throwing punches, I would bop the sweet spot and it was goodnight, sweet Lucy. The friends standing by, cheerleading, would look at me in disbelief and part like the Red Sea when I walked right through them, removing my gear.

As the date of my first fight approached, I assumed I was going to fight in the novice division. That's the beginner level. I'd only been sparring and I had no experience in a real fight yet, so I figured Rocky would abide by the rules and fight me with a kid who had five fights or under. I kept hearing from other, more experienced, fighters that it was different to fight under the lights, with a roaring crowd. These comments had a way of reaching into the back of my mind and turning the insecurity and anxiety dials all the way up. I hardly slept the night before the fight. I thought my nervousness was a sign of cowardice. I didn't have the guts to tell Rocky that his killer protégé was so terrified. I figured I would lose all of the newfound love and respect he held for his young lion. Now I know that I was not only nervous for that fight, but for every single fight that I've ever had. It's a completely healthy to feel the fight-or-flight response. It keeps you sharp, and it's how you use it that determines the final outcome.

As we made the forty-five minute drive to Las Cruces, New Mexico, I can remember lying in the fetal position, anticipating the fight ahead. It was the most uncomfortable, nerve-racking drive I had ever taken. Rocky drove calmly, humming to 1950s songs on the radio while my knees were shaking and my hands were clammy. I was starting to feel that old feeling come back, with the *I don't want to do this anymore* affirmations repeating circuitously through my mind. Doubts started creeping back, just like the old times in junior high.

After what seemed like an eternity, we arrived at the festival that was hosting the fights. We walked up to the front desk to register and let them know we needed to be counted.

The lady at the front said, "Okay, so we have him fighting open class, correct?"

Rocky replied, "Yes, that's right. We will fight anyone."

I looked at him with eyes that said, *What the fuck? Excuse me, but open class?* Open class means you've had over ten fights. I told Rocky, "Are you crazy, old man? I'm barely a novice!"

He just said, "Don't let me down."

I couldn't believe it. I felt like he betrayed me. He grabbed my gear and robe and told me to follow him outside. The fights were being held outside. It was a yearly festival called "The Great Enchilada Festival." As we walked through the double doors to go to our dressing room, I saw the crowd. It had to be at least three thousand people. I could see the big bright glare that was beaming off the trophies showcased next to the ring. I stopped following Rocky and stared at the spectacle in complete awe. I couldn't believe I was about to have my first real fight and I was scared out of my mind. Rocky yelled over at me and signaled me over to the dressing room. He made me lay down on the floor with my feet up on a chair to rest my nervous legs and conserve energy. I still had no idea who I was going to fight. I laid on the floor silently wondering who this mystery kid could be. I wondered if he was as nervous or as scared as I was.

Then, as I was just about to listen to music on my Walk-man, a representative walked into our dressing area and pulled Rocky aside. "You understand your kid is a novice. The only other kid we have in his weight division is the Junior Olympic Champion with over 300 fights. Would you like to go ahead and pull him out of this fight?"

He laughed out loud and said, "Hell, no. This kid I have is special."

I couldn't believe what I'd heard. Does he want me killed or crippled? All the confidence I acquired in the last few months just got zapped out of me. Once again, I was a scared little boy. I laid motionless and frozen until the official finally walked back into our room and said, "You got twenty minutes and you're on, kid."

A shot of adrenaline went rushing through my veins. This wasn't practice anymore. This was about to get real. Rocky quickly wrapped up my hands and I started hitting the mitts with him. The echoes from the pops of the mitt drill were cause for immediate attention. People would walk by my dressing room just to listen and peek in on my performance. I was used to that kind of response. I knew I was impressive, but I was still scared out of my mind.

After I had been warming up for a few minutes, another official walked into our dressing room and said, "Okay, fellas, it's fight time! Let's go ahead and get out there! People have been waiting for this one!"

We made our way out from the dressing room and started our walk to the boxing ring. All I could hear were the loud cheers and all I could see was the brightness of the sun in my eyes. People gathered around my entrance and began patting me on the back and slapping my gloves as I approached closer and closer to the ring. I walked up the stairs and climbed through the ropes. I glanced around at the large spectacle of the crowd and saw a sea of unfamiliar faces yelling and cheering for me. It was surreal. I was light-headed and couldn't feel my legs. I was overloaded with adrenaline. My breathing was shallow, pupils dilated.

The announcer came to the center of the ring to introduce the both of us. I hesitated, lifting one arm up after he managed to mispronounce my name, but I went along with it. The cheers were subtle and I even heard some distracting boos. Then he announced the other kid and before he could complete his full name, the stands were in an uproar and cheering. The referee asked both of us to the center of the ring and gave us the instruction briefly once more. We glared into each other's eyes hatefully. The referee said, "Protect yourself at all times and let's make this a good fight, fellas!"

Holy shit. Here we go.

I slowly walked back to my corner and started bouncing around like I'd seen the fighters do on television. Then out of nowhere I heard a real loud DING! DING! DING! The referee signaled us to come out punching. BAM! BAM! BOOM!!! We traded blows in barrages. We were both connecting and we both had fire in our eyes. I could hear the echoes of the crowd going wild. I couldn't understand it. I was wearing smaller gloves and this guy was just taking my punches. I started to see a little blood come out of his nose and then I felt a BLAAAM!

He caught me with a horrendous shot that almost knocked me out. I was dizzy and I couldn't make sense of my surroundings. I somehow kept my balance and kept up exchanging punches, except now I had blood pouring down my throat. I could feel my lungs struggle for fresh oxygen. It was right about then that his experience started to show. He was giving me a ride to school with his foot pressed on the gas. I became desperate and started missing my punches. He pressed forward and timed my punches. He'd let me miss and then pop-shot me with three to five punches at a time. I was in unfamiliar territory and counting down the seconds of the round in my head. I needed the bell, but it must have forgotten to ring. This round was lasting an eternity. I was outclassed and feeling humiliated. I could see out of my peripheral vision that the referee was about to step in and wave it off.

Finally the bell rang. I stumbled back to my corner, tired and disoriented, and sat down on the stool. Rocky was giving me instruction but I heard nothing. I could just feel the cold mist of water being sprayed on me as I gasped for whatever oxygen I could get. I was done. There was no way I could get back out there for another three minutes. This kid was just too good and I had absolutely nothing left in the tank.

The ten-second whistle blew for us to get off our stools and be ready to answer the bell. I looked across to the opposing corner and could see the kid patiently listening to one final instruction from his trainer with an enormous grin. *Did he just fucking grin? This motherfucker just grinned at me! He thinks I'm a joke?* I got mad and laser-focused. I thought, *fuck this guy.* The bell rang and he charged out at me like his corner had told him to, and then BAM! My vicious left hook caught him. He dropped headfirst and was out dead cold. *Goodnight, motherfucker. Sweet dreams.*

He struggled and strained to get up, but his effort wasn't enough and he fell against the referee. I saw his nose was badly broken and his eyes were glazed over. It was only ten seconds into the second round.

I heard silence in the crowd and then a huge roar. I felt so amazing that I jumped up and kissed the sky. Rocky leapt into the ring and tried picking me up, but after trying and failing, a high-five was good enough. We hugged and I cried. I couldn't believe that I had just knocked out one of the best guys in the amateurs and it was only my first fight. This kid came all the way from East Los Angeles looking for a quick tune-up win, and instead he got delivered a stunning upset.

I gazed at my trophy the whole way home and talked with Rocky. We talked about what we would do when I became Champion of the World and the places we would travel. It was and still is the most magical moment of my life. I was full of hope and excitement instead of humility and depression. When we got back to El Paso, he announced me to his bar as his future champ and had me give a small speech on the band stage. He even let me drink a little that night, just as long as I stayed on his couch at his home. His home was conveniently located ten feet across the alley from the bar.

My hangover the next day was accompanied by tremendous soreness, due to the blows to my head. All that was easily ignored because I was staring at my first ever, most beautiful trophy. I hugged and kissed it. It was as if boxing had given birth to my first child. It was a symbol of conquering my fears and overcoming my darkest demons. Little did I know that the devil is wise, and that this would be the first of many tests to come, inside and outside the ring.

CHAPTER 10

HIGH SCHOOL DROPOUT
WITH A PURPOSE

Another summer came and went, but school was no longer on the agenda for me. I was about to be a senior, but all I wanted to do was perfect my craft as a fighter. I knew my direction in life, and listening to the teachers nag at me day after day was wearing down my patience. I felt the studies were pointless and the homework was severely getting in the way of my training regime. Having to go home after exhausting workouts so I could worry about reading some pointless book chapter that I would forget in a few weeks was no longer on my agenda. Boxing was using up every last ounce of my mental and physical energy. I was going to be the champion of the world and I had no intention to ever go back. I'd rather get up and run in the early mornings instead of worrying about being tardy for some school bell. I'd rather head off in the evenings and train with Rocky instead of being cooped up in after-school detention. I'd rather learn to fight and build a legacy instead of learning to be some working stiff who hates his job.

The more I thought about it, school was starting to make less and less sense. I decided I wasn't going to go back—maybe I'd go back for lunch with friends, but screw all the regular classes. There was just one minor thing bugging me, though: I didn't want to give my parents further heartbreak. I just had to figure out a way to train and get the grades.

I spoke with a kid at the boxing gym who told me about a test called the GED. I was amazed that you could fast track and simply pass a generic test for high school; it sounded too good to be true, but I was 100% into it. This way, my parents could be proud that I graduated, while the teachers could kiss my ass. I didn't tell my parents about my decision because I figured I would pass the test and then proudly hand them the diploma. I went to the office the next day and told them all to kiss my big white ass while mooning the front receptionists. I remember the bewildered look on the faces of the faculty staff. Women broke out in laughter as I ran out the front metal doors trying to pull up my jeans and underwear. Why would a kid make it all the way to senior year and then drop out? It made no sense to them, and it doesn't make any sense to me now, but I was a kid and I believed in my mission.

As I ran out of the front doors of Coronado High School to freedom, I went directly to enroll in the GED classes. This was going to be a breeze, I thought to myself. I drove to the alternative school and registered in the fast-track program. The next week I was scheduled to start my classes. These classes would allow me to train due to the shorter days; most of the kids in the program had jobs and worked half the day. I had Rocky sign a waiver that I worked at his bar as a janitor. I walked into the class the first day and took a long, panoramic gaze around the classroom. It was quiet and these kids looked like they were really struggling with the material they were given. The teacher pointed to an empty desk and told me to sit down. He wanted to do a baseline test and see where my weaknesses were in the desired subjects that he chose. He began to deliver one practice test after another. I aced each one, handing them in with haste and a smile. The other students looked at me like I was mocking them, but I wasn't. I just wanted to get to the gym and this shit was too easy. The teacher would stare at me with a sarcastic smile and shake his head as if knowing my answers had to be wrong. I completed all the baseline tests in a record two days. If I passed, I would be given the GED test, or I'd be told that I would have to take some short classes on the subjects I was weak in. Either way, in my youth and inexperience, I figured it was better than regular schooling.

On my third day of walking into the GED program, the teacher pulled me aside and said, "Why are you going to waste such a brilliant mind and go get hit in the head for a living, son?" I felt as if he had just blatantly insulted me and my life's mission. "Sorry sir, but I'm taking this test because I'm on my way to greatness and I don't want to be like you, working behind a desk." He just shook his head, made a disgruntled sound under his breath, and handed me the official test. I thought the test at first was a complete joke. *How could any kid in this classroom be struggling with this*, I thought to myself. I even walked up to the teacher and asked if he was certain he gave me the correct test. I thought it may have been another practice test. I completed the test in record time and ran up to the desk to watch him grade it with his special infrared glasses. After giving me my official grade, he pleaded with me to go back to high school. He then grinned and told me I had passed it better than any kid in there in last five years. He told me how kids have been in the GED program for six months and still couldn't pass. I laughed sarcastically and replied, "Why don't they just go back to school, then?" I'm surprised he didn't slap my wise-ass across the mouth for that little sarcastic statement.

I was just a child, and I was exuberant with artificial confidence about my life. I knew better than all the teachers and all my elders. This is something that still haunts me, and probably will for the remainder of my adult life. My objective was to get in and get out within a week, and I accomplished that. These other kids wasting months for a simple test should just get their asses back in school, I thought to myself. In hindsight, I didn't take into consideration that maybe they couldn't because they had behavioral problems, or that maybe they had new, young families. Maybe this was the only way to get ahead in life so they could get a real paying job, and quickly.

I walked into my house proudly, chin up, GED diploma in hand. I wanted my father to embrace me and feel proud. I wanted to hear his laughter as he looked over my freshly-inked diploma with pride. I wanted my mother to begin weeping in celebration as she promised to frame my accomplishment. I ended my graduation walk into my house and smiled while handing him the rolled paper. He said, "What's this, son?" I said, "It's my diploma, dad." He slowly took it out of my hand as I stood there, still smiling. He opened it up and read it over with his reading glasses. I was waiting in anticipation and excitement for his response of joy and glee.

After a few moments of reading the generic diploma, he looked at me in disappointment and threw it onto the table along with the morning newspaper. He then walked off, shaking his head in confusion. My heart dropped with devastation. I had just destroyed my mother's and father's hearts once more. I hated disappointing my father because I looked up to him so much and wanted his approval.

Shortly after his display of discontent, my father looked me at the only way a father knows how and consoled me. He knew I had made up my mind and he told me he would stand behind me on any venture I chose. The relief I felt after our conversation allowed me to look ahead once more to my future. I told my father that in his honor that I would win every fight from that day forward. I really didn't understand how much unrealistic pressure I was putting on myself.

Shortly after dropping out, my days consisted of running the mountain terrain in the mornings, resting up in the afternoons, and then off to the boxing gym in the evenings. Rocky and I worked hard every day toward a dream with endless possibilities. We both had visions of championships and glory. We had to take the first step by bringing some amateur titles back home.

CHAPTER 11

THE MURDER OF MY MENTOR

Rocky

I t was a day that started off as every routine day did. I woke up early, ate a healthy breakfast, did my run, and was resting up before I hit the gym. I called Rocky a few times, but there was no answer. He was supposed to have new sparring ready for me on this particular day. It wasn't too unusual that he didn't answer, so I put my gear together to head off for practice. I drove my dad's big, blue Lincoln town car with the tinted windows. It was a total baller status car and I loved driving it. I also used to love how the tires would grip the asphalt when I did donuts in my high school parking lot. At that age, I was always in a hurry to go everywhere. I was that annoying, obnoxious kid driving ninety miles an hour, weaving in and out of traffic. I was in such a rush for nothing. As I raced like I always did to the gym to get the workout started, I pulled up to Rocky's bar and it was closed. That was odd, but it was even stranger that there wasn't a single soul around. I would usually roll up to the bar and gym and there would be two sets of music blasting, loud Tejano music from the inside of the bar and hip hop blasting from the back, where the gym was located.

As I grabbed my gear and went around back, I had to hop over the gate because the door was locked. I was in such a hurry to get warmed up, I still thought nothing of it. I plugged in the beat-up FM stereo while carefully wrapping my hands for the workout. We didn't have cell phones back then, so I had to walk around the bar and gym yelling Rocky's name. I noticed his Cadillac parked at his house next door. After a long time spent screaming his name, I decided to go ahead and start warming up. I figured he must have walked over to the neighborhood grocery store to buy his daily fruits and vegetables. He usually walked over to the market to buy the fresh fruit that was delivered in the morning. It wasn't irregular to watch him peel an orange while giving instruction.

After about forty-five minutes of working out by myself, I started to get irritated that he wasn't there on time to work with me. I decided to stop my workout and walk over to his place to see what exactly was going on, so I hopped the locked gate and marched to his house sweaty, frustrated, and angry. As I approached the house, I felt an eerie presence, like a tangible silence, surrounding it. I hesitated, but still walked up to the front door and started knocking repetitively. I yelled his name, "Rocky! Hey Rocky... Hello? Rocky!" No answer. I decided to go around the back of the house and try my obnoxiously loud knocking again. I shouted his name and peered into his windows, but the shades were drawn down. I couldn't see anything and I felt uneasy. None of this made any sense. I sat on his back porch and contemplated what my next move would be. I decided that I would just go home and hope to hear from him that evening. I started to leave, but knocked once again for good measure. No answer.

I went back to the gym and gathered my gear. I was confused and upset. I threw my gear in the trunk of the Town Car and decided to peel out in front of his house in case he was in there and could hear me. I wanted him to know I was angry. For the first time I went home after a workout disgruntled and unsatisfied. Usually I felt complete and content after a hard day's routine.

After hours of waiting to hear from him, I started to get nervous. I started to feel knots form in my stomach, the kind you feel when you instinctively know something just isn't right.

A few more hours went by. I had finished dinner when the phone rang. My mother yelled, "Davy! It's for you, it's Joe Sullivan. He says it's important!"

I grabbed the phone frantically, knowing something had to be wrong. I said, "Yeah, Joe, talk to me."

I sat in silence as he spoke calmly and directly. I listened as my world went into a slow-motion train wreck and my throat began to close. My reality started to fade in and out like I was hallucinating, but without the psychedelics. My hands got clammy. My knees started to buckle. I had no balance. It was like I was got hit with a right hook by Tyson. I lost my grip on the phone and it fell to the floor. I laid there for a few minutes as my world started spinning. I couldn't move. The walls were closing in on me.

I could hear Joe's voice on the phone as it laid across from me, "Dave, hello? Dave, just get down here to the bar, man. Maybe you can help answer some questions."

After hearing those muffled words in the distance, I pulled myself up in a shock and grabbed my father's car keys. My mentor and hero was dead and it was looking like a homicide. As I arrived at the bar, I pulled up to five police cars and an ambulance. There was yellow crime scene tape sealing his home. Forensic teams were outside, cautiously dusting for fingerprints. I stepped out from the car in a daze and in disbelief.

Joe slowly walked over to me. He said words, but I heard nothing. I just saw his mouth moving with concern upon his face. I could only hear that they had found him lying on his bed with his head blown off. His son had come over and couldn't get into Rocky's house, so he called the cops to assist in his entry. The story played over and over in my mind. Adrenaline was rushing all through my body as I kept trying to get a glimpse of the massacre inside. A strange and curious part of me just had to see what happened to Rocky. Maybe I could see something in the house that wasn't right or could add some help in the matter. I had to see if this was even real. When you love and care for somebody, you just want to be with them one last time. It doesn't matter what condition they're in.

Joe and a few other cops ran over and stopped me before I could reach the inside of the house. Joe didn't want my last memory of Rocky to be of the horror, the gore and blood. After trying to struggle and fight my way through, I was in no condition to drive. The cops asked Joe if he would escort me home. He obliged and hugged me as we both began crying. He then put his arm around my shoulders like the older brother he had been to me and walked me back to my car. I gave him the keys and we both got in and shut the doors in silence. The silence lasted four seconds until we both broke down again. The pain disappeared and I went numb. I stared out the window as we drove off, wondering what would become of my life without Rocky. What would Rocky tell me to do in this moment?

During the silent and macabre ride home I just gazed out at the other cars we were passing on the freeway, wondering why we live in a world of such heartache and pain. If there was a God, why did he take away my only promise in life, and why so brutally? Why take away someone I cared for in an act of brutal murder? When we finally got to my house, I ran inside and hugged my parents. Tears ran down my face as they held and consoled me. My dad threw his hands to the side and said with a respectful nod, "That crazy fucking Rocky. God bless him." He sat down, quietly surrendering himself to his favorite spot on the couch, and stared off intensely, contemplating the heart-wrenching news in silence.

The funeral was a week later and I was supposed to be a pallbearer. I'd never been one before, and I didn't like the act of having to carry a loved one to their final resting place. It made me uncomfortable and I cringed inside, but it was the right thing to do. After all, he was the man that gave me confidence and carried my insecurity upon his shoulders. He was always in my corner and he made this little boy become a man. It was only fitting that I would help carry him to his final resting place. The funeral was beautiful and it seemed half of the city came out to pay their last respects to "the old Bowie Bear, and great boxing legend."

I saw and spoke to so many people at the funeral whose lives he had touched and forever altered. So many kids were there showing support, and I felt as if a knife was going through me every time I saw his son, Joe, break down in uncontrollable tears. It was unbearable to watch. Rocky was known to have his harem of girlfriends, and at the funeral, they came out in droves. He was obviously a very busy man and that's what caused all the trouble. In the end, it was a jealous woman. After months of investigation, it was discovered that Rocky was killed with a shotgun to the head by a jealous and spiteful ex-girlfriend. She had shot him with a pillow covering his head while he was asleep.

After Rocky's death, the direction of my life changed once more, but this time, I had no idea where I was going. I was a scared little boy with nothing but fear erupting inside me. So I did what any raging hormonal teenager would do. I decided to rebel and make God pay for his acts of vengeance upon my life. The ultimate prank of life was on me, and I was a troubled and lost cause. My days of dedication to boxing and living for a stupid pipe dream were over. Now it was time to throw all my cares away, get into some good, fun trouble and do whatever the hell I wanted.

CHAPTER 12

SPIRALING DOWN THE DRAIN

After Rocky's death, I free-fell into a deep and dark depression. Not only because I had lost a loved one and mentor, but because at Rocky's funeral it felt as if I had to bury my dream of boxing. I didn't trust any of the other coaches in the El Paso area and I had a certain pride in training at Rocky's Bar and Gym. It was always Rocky's misfits against the rest of the El Paso boxing clubs. We had a special mystique that followed us. It fueled our fire to train every day, knowing that other gyms didn't approve of our methods and despised us.

Rocky had a respected old-school belief system that kept his fighters mean, nasty, and hungry. We trained as Spartans or modern day gladiators. He hammered his rules into our heads: no sex before fights, and no girlfriends because they make you soft. No women were ever allowed into his gym. He referred to it as the Spartans' boxing sanctuary. It was our church and his rules were our religion. We quickly learned to adopt these rules and methods and we never asked any questions. If I was seeing a certain girl, I would never bring her to the gym. It was totally frowned upon. To this day I still keep that habit. I never allow a girlfriend to watch me train at the gym, nor will I train when women are in the gym. I feel it's no place for them and they cause distraction. I'm a firm believer in keeping your fighting senses strict and killer instinct sharp. Having women around when you're training or getting ready for a fight changes the dynamic, dulls the killer instinct. I always go into the ring ready to kill and destroy a motherfucker with no sense of mercy; and as Rocky always said, "A lion can't hunt with his dick hard." When I started going to other gyms later in life, I purposefully went when no females would be there. I found it embarrassing to have to watch them in the gym, training with males. I felt it was subconsciously making the men weak. In fighting you must continuously keep up the process of sharpening your blade, because soft habits lead to hard losses. Many of the great fighters still practice this philosophy and train privately.

As the months went by, I kept falling deeper into my depression with no real end in sight. The depression would get so dark on some days, that I would refuse to get out of bed. It was easier to stay within the confines of my bedroom and continue soaking in my sorrowful slumber. I saw no way to fix my problems and I felt my dream died along with Rocky. I had no idea what to do about it, so I went back to what I knew would make me feel better temporarily, my two best friends in crises—drugs and alcohol. I knew it was wrong, but fuck it, I felt terrible and every day I was becoming more and more suicidal. I needed an escape and drinking provided a feeling of detachment. I thought I couldn't let go of Rocky's death sober, and alcohol provided the temporary solution.

I started going out every night with my friends and somehow I believed that I deserved to have some good old-fashioned fun. You're only young once, is what I would always repeat to the constant naysayers or my concerned parents. I needed a replacement. I needed to fill that empty void where the stimulation of living for a dream of championship glory once resided. I needed a solution and I needed it fast. Alcohol and drugs became the obvious answer. What made this temporary solution even more dangerous was the fact that I needed to somehow combine it with the stimulation and adrenaline that I could only receive in the boxing ring. It started with the fights in bars, and constant one night stands while alcohol drowned my sorrows. I was notching up about a fight per week while sending some poor sucker into la-la land. Many nights I would come home with swollen and badly cut knuckles from some sucker's teeth I volunteered to shatter.

About three nights a week we'd cross over to Juárez and I'd drink until I couldn't see straight. I'd get into a few fights, then get arrested and then thrown in Mexican jail. I was sleeping with so many different girls that I could choose the richest daddy's girl to come bail me out of my Mexican dilemma. It was an understood routine for these girls, and even though they complained about it, they were no match for my evil charm and disarming smile. I was just too damn good at getting my selfish and self-destructive way. Drowning alone was too scary for my cowardly and childish character.

One night is still firmly etched within my memory bank. It was epic, and to this day it's legendary among certain friends. In Juárez, I was kissing a girl at the notorious Tequila Derby nightclub and bar when a jealous punk kid walked by and knocked my Corona over, spilling it all over me and my new flavor of that night. He stared at me with his best impression of an intimidating gaze and cursed at me in Spanish. I couldn't exactly make out what he was saying, so I leaned in and said, "*Que puto?*" He picked up the empty Corona bottle and beamed it right at my face. I felt the breeze whisk past, whistling like a bottle rocket across my ear.

My boxing reflexes must have still been sharp even in my drunken and slumbering state. Right after I dodged the bottle, I reeled back and cracked him on his jaw. He collapsed in front of me like I shot him with a taser. I stared at him as he twisted and flopped with convulsions. I felt someone's big, heavy arm go around the base of my neck, choking the life out from me.

As my eyes rolled into the back of my head, I started to go unconscious and slip away. In my peripheral vision I could vaguely see my friend Danny come running to my rescue. He started delivering relentless punches to whoever had the death grip on me. Danny used to like to make the most ridiculous sound effects when he punched people. "BAM BOOM BAM, bitch!" That was Danny's signature three-punch calling card, and the poor bastard that was choking me let go immediately. The man fell to his knees and hands while Danny and I both took turns kicking him in the ribs and face. We quickly knocked out his teeth and we didn't stop at that. As this sorry bastard was begging and pleading for his life, Danny decided to grab a pool stick and beat him senseless with it. I witnessed strike after strike as the man tried to cover and protect his face with limited to no success. This senseless rampage persisted until the club bouncers ran up to us in horror, holding up chairs like lion tamers.

Then my other friend Sammy, who we affectionately referred to as "The Bull," came running out the of crowd, punching one of the bouncers holding up a chair. Sammy was even wearing a cast on his left hand from a street fight he was in the previous weekend. Next thing I knew, the whole bar had broken out into a frenzy and tables and chairs were flying.

Screams and yells were deafening my ears. People were even picking up bottles and throwing them at us. They were doing anything to try and stop the mayhem that had broken out. I realized that Danny, Sammy, and I were fighting the whole damn bar. Punches and kicks were being thrown from every angle. I started to bleed out of my nose and my right eye was swollen shut. I had one guy by his shirt, punching his face, while another bouncer was hitting me on the right side of my face with a mag steel flashlight. I could hear nothing, but I felt the vibration and occasional ringing of my skull as he continued with the relentless strikes on my dome. I started to feel the warm blood pour down my neck and shoulders.

As we endured the hits, we tried to make our way to the front entrance. We started tearing up and coughing relentlessly. Our throats began to close, making breathing impossible. I looked to my left and saw a heavyset bouncer unloading a can of pepper spray onto the whole bar to stop the chaos from going any further. The bar was already badly damaged and pieces of the tables and chairs were scattered all over the bloodstained floor. People started to clear out. Everyone was running for the exits and we were no exception. We felt our way through the herds of people with what poor vision we had left. Sheer terror and panic overcame my mind and body in the middle of all this madness.

As we made it out of the entrance, thinking we were home free, I felt my body slam hard against the outside pavement. My face was pressed against the sidewalk with the sharp prod of a knee in my shoulder blades. As my eyes veered up, I made out the silhouette of a Juárez *Federale*. He pointed a machine gun at my head and yelled at me in Spanish. I just froze. He gave a signal for me to stand up. I rose to my feet while he kept the machine gun pointed between my eyes.

Then the bouncers ran outside and pointed at me, yelling, "*Si! Este Huey!! Este pinche Huey!!*" I knew I was in serious trouble and I looked around desperately for an escape. I wasn't getting out of this one, no way in hell.

As the Federale called for backup over radio dispatch, he reached around his back to ready his handcuffs so that he could cuff me. As all hope began to dwindle from me, I heard a "BOOM BOOM BOOM, BITCH!" It was the sweet sound of good ole Danny's calling card. As the Mexican cop hit the floor, he started to crawl toward his machine gun. That's when I ran over to him and pushed him back over on his side. I ran and kicked his gun even further down the curb into the street full of traffic.

Danny yelled, "Run, bro! Let's go, man!" I knew we were dead if we didn't. We took off in a dead heat, zig-zagging through the congested traffic of Juárez. We knew the only hope we had was to make it to the bridge and run like hell to the American side. That was our only goal. While we ran, we were both still choking and coughing, and our vision was impaired by the effects of the pepper spray. All we could hear were the footsteps pounding behind us as the traffic came to screeching and halting stops. I even hit and flew over one of the cars, destroying the windshield, but when adrenaline is pumping to save your life, nothing will stop you.

As freedom approached, we kicked it into high gear one last time, like it was an NFL combined tryout. We sprinted and jumped over the gate and ran even faster up the bridge. The yells and screams from the bouncers and Mexican police started falling more and more distant behind us. We were finally home free. As we slowed down, our lungs burned. Once we felt it was safe, we stopped for the impossible task of catching our breath. We both bent over and puked uncontrollably.

Once we made it to the El Paso side in the dawn twilight, there were big puddles from the previous night's rain all over the filthy streets of the downtown area. We didn't hesitate before running to the closest puddle and splashing our eyes and faces frantically. We had to get that pepper spray out. When you're in that much pain and feeling that desperate, you'll do anything. I can still remember the taste of oil and dirt residue from that blackened street puddle. It was filthy.

Once the burning and choking stopped temporarily, we looked at each other quietly for a few seconds before screaming, "FUCK YEAH! Did you see that? Did you see me do this? Did you see me do that? Oh my God! I can't believe we made it!" We celebrated our mad dash to freedom. We could have disappeared into a Mexican jail cell, or worse. We could even have been shot dead. We jumped up and down celebrating for what seemed like a good twenty minutes, giving each other high-fives while theatrically rerunning the fight in our minds.

I said, "Man, we can't go back for at least a week, bro."

He looked at me sarcastically and said, "Nah, bro, just a few days. There are other clubs on the strip we can hit." That was honestly our thought process. We were complete idiots.

It wasn't any longer than two weeks before we all decided to give in to the temptation. We went to a few desert bonfire parties to kill some time, but that didn't give me or my friends the rush that the Juárez nightlife could deliver. So many good-looking girls, fights, and drinks could not be turned down. It was too tempting and we, as young men, couldn't resist the dangling carrot. We went back, risking everything. I was a wound-up ball of nerves when I went back for the first time, but to my astonishment, when we returned to the strip, we were greeted with open arms by most of the club owners.

We didn't set foot in the Tequila Derby, but we definitely hit all the other major bars and clubs on the strip.

All the owners loved us, the only reason being that we put money in their pockets. We were good for the clubs and we were good for their economy. We would throw the big killer parties every weekend that brought in the rich west side kids. We brought them gold and they couldn't afford to lose us. One little mishap was forgivable and could be excused. We were notorious for throwing the big parties, and everybody made good money. They would charge at the door, "five dollar drink and drown," and usually give us a kickback of a buck a head. We could make anywhere between $500 to $2000 a weekend. Remember, this was an economy fueled by American high school kids. American kids would pour into Juárez from all over El Paso to party at the destinations we had chosen for that weekend. We would go talk to a specific club owner the week before and plan for a party in a place of our choosing. We would then go print up thousands of flyers and promote the hell out of our party at high schools all over the city. It was our guerilla marketing tactics that secured a party and some spending money for us every weekend. We would hit all the major high schools with mounds of flyers. Instead of putting them on car windshields every Friday, we would just cruise into the high school parking lots and dump brightly colored flyers all over the school grounds. High school kids came out every Friday to messes of flyers all over their parking lots.

After a couple of years of this constant routine of being drunk almost every weekend, I started to feel that deep void again. Street fights, drinking, and girls were only a bandage masking a deeper pain. I still felt empty inside, like I had no meaning or purpose. I definitely didn't believe in God any more. I believed that the universe was just made up of random acts and chaotic messes. My emptiness and depression had depended upon the worship at three altars: women, parties, and alcohol. They were just temporary fixes, but they deadened the pain I felt inside until the hideous feeling of being sober resurrected itself.

I knew I had a few things going for me outside of boxing. I could make people laugh, I could out-drink almost anyone my age, and I was a charming, great-looking guy that could talk the panties off almost any girl in the right atmosphere. Rare were the nights that I didn't succeed. I can't count the number of times I met a girl at a club and took her to the restroom to have sex, while making a few others wait until I finished. I was a completely jaded individual and eventually it got to a point where I would have sex with different women two to four times any given night. My friends would joke and tell me that this behavior wasn't remotely normal, but it was my religion. Anybody who told me different didn't have the game or the confidence that I had, so I really didn't care for their sheepish opinions. I was a wolf and I craved the taste of lamb chops. They were only mad because I didn't have to hunt for it. I would go out to the pasture and take my pick of sheep. It had literally become a buffet of sex.

Still, I couldn't hide that I was empty. The void became too deep. The vicious cycle was women, drugs, alcohol, and now a fourth demon—suicidal thoughts. I would wake up some mornings and stare down into the barrel of a nice, shiny Glock .45 that I had bought a few years prior on the black market. I would get ready to pull the trigger, and then the thought of my dear, beautiful mother crying would put a halt to that. I would drop the gun and begin to cry over what my life had become. I had gone through my whole young life breaking her heart. I couldn't just selfishly take the life that my parents proudly gave me, just because I was unhappy and depressed.

Eventually, after considerable counseling, I realized that I couldn't take the easy and cowardly way out. I had to think of another option. I had to vent my depression and anger on something else. I had to go back to what I knew. I had to get back into boxing, even if that meant doing it without my mentor, Rocky. I desperately needed something to save my life.

CHAPTER 13

LIGHTING THE SPARK . . . AGAIN

It could have been another chance encounter, but I prefer to think of it as divine intervention. The day finally came when I got sick of feeling sorry for myself, so I rolled my lethargic, depressed ass out of bed. I decided it was time to do something, anything. I knew I needed physical activity to cure the depression hangover. I had to get into some kind of routine, at the very least lift some weights and blow off some steam. I hit the only gym I was a member of, the local, run-down YMCA. I went there because my dad loved to play racquetball three times a week and I was on his family membership. The YMCA mainly had racquetball courts, but there was a small weight room and sauna. The sauna was the place I never went into, because it had a reputation as a homosexual hook-up spot where men would signal each other for sex acts, like a first base coach throwing hand signals at his player. If you got the signal, you would probably get screwed, and I mean that literally. A fresh, pretty boy like me took no chances.

After a few a weeks of lifting weights and seeing my progress, I decided I would start going there routinely to try and kill my depression and boredom. It was a real dumpy looking place, but I loved it. The entrance smelt of mothballs and you could hear the sounds of the players' tennis shoes screeching on the basketball court as you walked in. The weight room had rusty machinery and a nostalgic 1960s sense to it. It was like they got their machinery in bulk, for a killer cheap deal, at an outside junk yard. The equipment was severely outdated and could probably kill somebody if not properly used. It was simply plates, chains and pulleys. Half the time one of machines would be broken, or there would be a line of two or three individuals waiting to use the bench press. Guys would stand in line cranking out push-ups until they were next up to use the bench. It had much the feel of a prison yard to it.

I began a routine where I'd go into the aerobics room, which was next to the weight room, and shadowbox for thirty minutes straight to work up a sweat. I would follow that up with twenty minutes of jump rope to cool down. When I finished that, I would head into the weight room and let my muscles swell as I pressed the weights for at least an hour. I was new to weights and I couldn't believe how fast my body responded. Every week I was growing and getting stronger. I would eat like a horse and continue the routine the next day. I just had too much excess energy to burn. I had no idea where my life was going, but I knew I couldn't lie in bed all day. I knew my life needed a change and I had to start somewhere. I also returned to the habit of praying every day, because maybe I was wrong and there was a God. Maybe if He was up there, He would pick up on one of my signals of distress and come help me out.

This routine lasted for weeks and I remained hopeful. I put a couple of job applications in, but I soon figured out that I could make money so much easier by going to Juárez and buying steroids for all the muscle heads in the weight room. I would hike up the price 50-75% for these muscle-head goons. I made quick, easy money, but it was too risky. Crossing over the bridge weekly, my pants loaded up with steroid cartridges, was only making me a nervous wreck. After a few weeks of this little side business, I folded under the pressure and decided to retire from my short career as a drug smuggler.

I desperately needed some kind of savior to come into my life. I began working out hard and praying even harder. One night, my prayers hit the right mailbox. I put all my worries into God's hands and decided to get on my knees and pray. I must have prayed for thirty minutes in tears. I prayed and flooded my pillows with tears and I put myself to sleep. I woke the next day and went about my usual routine.

On that particular day, a boxing promoter we referred to as "Big Jon" strolled into the YMCA with his prized professional heavyweight boxer of the time. They wanted to get in a quick workout before they headed up to Ruidoso, New Mexico for a high-altitude training camp in the mountains. I watched in complete awe as this heavyweight boxer shadow-boxed at the mirror. Every time he punched, he had perfect technique and, for a big man, a sleek finesse. He had a strong, solid build that looked like he was etched from stone. His name was Jimmy Thunder.

Big Jon would stand by his side, yelling instructions and reaffirming his work with positive affirmations. Jon was a tall, burly man who sported a Kenny Rogers beard with tints of red and gray. He was from the Midwest, and he was a used car salesman that happened to find his love and niche in the boxing world. He could talk circles around anybody and before you knew it, you were hustled. He had a Midwest accent and reminded me of a Waylon Jennings-esque good ole boy. He was charismatic and hilarious with a trove of backwoods expressions and vulgar jokes.

As I watched from a distance, I decided that I would make myself noticeable. I stood in the back, watching Jimmy Thunder throw thunderous punches at the mirror. I knew Jon saw me watching as he gave the push for his heavyweight to work out even harder. I started to get the sense that he recognized me, too. I'd heard stories that he used to hang out with my dad and his friends back in the good old days. All those men in their prime were a bunch of rough and tough, rowdy troublemakers and they all drank and played poker together.

As I was busy watching in intimidation yet admiration, Jon glanced over at me and said, "You're David's little boy, aren't you, son?"

I said, "Yes sir, I am."

He laughed loudly and shook his head. He followed up with a long, funny story about how he hung out with my father and the trouble they once got into. It hit way too close to home for me, but at that moment it made me realize that maybe that's why my dad was always a little lenient with me—he used to do the same type of bullshit. After he finished his story, I burst out into laughter. That was the effect Big Jon had on people. He could sell an Eskimo an ice cream pie with that one simple laugh that only a good car salesman recognizes.

As I chuckled, he said, "Son, didn't you once give it a go at boxing?"

I answered back with, "Yes, I did, but chasing pussy and getting drunk served me a little more purpose, sir."

He replied, "Well, why don't you come up to camp with the rest of these heavyweights and get in some good sparring? Give it a go again?"

All I knew was that I wanted the hell out of El Paso. To

train with the same guys that I looked up to on television? This was a no-brainer. I wasted no time and eagerly shook his hand in excitement. We made plans for me to get up to Ruidoso the next weekend. I immediately raced home and told my parents. They were worried about me, but I could tell they were happy I had finally found some kind of direction that didn't involve drugs or alcohol.

As the days of that week went by, I couldn't wait till the weekend. I was charged up with too much piss and vinegar. I was ready to start my life. I had finally found something to look forward to. A real direction. A real purpose. All I knew was that I needed to get started, and I ended up leaving on a Thursday instead of that Saturday. I knew that my room wouldn't be ready at the training camp until Saturday, but I would sleep in my car if I had to. I just wanted out of my parents' house and a change of scenery. The endless rolling hills of sand and baking heat waves had finally taken its final toll on me.

So I jumped into my rusted and sun-parched red Ford Taurus two days earlier than planned, and began the two-hour journey up the mountains to Ruidoso, New Mexico. That day was one of the most exciting days of my life. Maybe God did exist, and maybe He heard one of the many prayers that He had so often seemed to ignore. I was full of a new hope and a feeling of excitement that I hadn't felt in the years since Rocky's death.

CHAPTER 14

KEEPING UP WITH THE BIG DOGS

The scenery throughout the mountainous terrain and along the winding road was fitting. As the desert landscape changed gradually into brush, then to bushes and then to trees, it made me reflect on the changes of my young life and the growth I was enduring. Getting to the top of these mountains and joining a camp with the true professionals signified a clear landmark. It symbolized my growth and progress toward greener pastures. On that day, I was reminded to never give up on myself, because the light will always appear at the end of the tunnel during the darkest time.

After the breathtaking scenery of mountainous terrain, with the pine trees and winding rivers, I finally drove into Ruidoso. As I approached the address Jon gave me, I took notice of the area in which I would now be residing. Beautiful log cabins stood out in the forefront of my view, and the mystical wilderness of rolling mountain terrain accented the horizon. The smell of the log cabin chimney smoke overcame all of my senses as I breathed it into my lungs along with the fresh and crisp mountain air. It was truly a breathtaking and magical experience to breathe in the scenery and become one with what I was feeling emotionally.

As I looked for the street signs written on the napkin I was holding, I dipped down the canyon hill to the training camp house, and I couldn't believe my eyes. The house was massive. It was a hidden mansion tucked away in the forest. When I pulled into the gravel driveway, I could hear, in the not-too-far distance, the sound of a creek. Along with the sound of running water, I could hear the commotion of crickets and frogs in sync with one another. I turned off my engine, turned off the lights and sat for a moment, absorbing the beauty.

A BANG BANG on my windshield pulled me out of my reverie. "Come on, son, you'll freeze your balls off out here." It was Big Jon. As he walked away from my car he beckoned me to come inside. I popped open the trunk, grabbed my things, and followed him. The inside of this place was even more beautiful than the outside. It had a western, Santa Fe–styled theme with massive pillars of wood holding up the ceiling and, at the bar, there was a huge brass statue of George Foreman throwing a punch. Supposedly, Jon had a lot to do with George Foreman's comeback and he was very proud of that accomplishment. He led me up the stairs and showed me to the resting quarters. As he showed me the workings of my running toilet, he explained the house rules. When he felt he was finished discussing all the important matters pertaining to the house, he pointed to my bed. "You better get some rest, kiddo. You're getting up at 5 A.M. to run the mountains with the other fighters."

That hit me like a brick. What the hell did he mean, 5 A.M.? I don't wake up until 10 A.M. on a good day. I held in my questions and outrage and politely nodded in agreement. When he walked out of my room and shut the door behind him, reality smacked me across the face. I was in a real training camp with real professional fighters. This is where they separate the men from the boys. I could not wimp out in this kind of atmosphere. I would get sniffed out and eaten alive immediately. I had to keep a poker face for as long as I decided to stay here. I needed to show that I belonged. I laid down that night and tried my best to sleep. I couldn't. I was too nervous about the following day and what obstacles it held.

As I finally began to drift asleep, a loud BANG hit my door. It was the trainer. "Rise and shine, princess, you're running five miles up some serious shit today!" Lightning struck my being and I started to think that I might have made the biggest mistake of my young life. In a panic, I hurriedly put on my sweats along with my pathetic-looking running shoes. I had forgotten to buy new shoes, so I decided to use the old beat-up pair I used back when I was training with Rocky. My big toe protruded out of the front of my left tennis shoe. Both shoes had holes in the worn-out soles. As I walked down the stairs, all the fighters got a glimpse of my shoes and erupted in laughter at me. "He's gonna be freezing his balls off and quitting, coach!" "This kid's gonna get his cherry popped today!" "He shoulda stayed back home with his mommy and daddy." Those were just a few of the comments they hurled at me. I swallowed my pride and decided to tune them out. I grabbed my cup of coffee and drank it while wiping the sleep away from my tired eyes.

As we all went out to the front and piled in the car, I decided to pay attention to and emulate the best fighter in the camp, Johnny Thunder. I knew I had to do exactly what he did. I noticed he kept quiet and was very short with his words. He had a calmness about him, with a noticeably blank and vicious stare within his eyes. He didn't crack jokes or laugh much. He stayed serious and focused on his training at hand. As we arrived at the bottom of the mountain area we were about to run, he took no time in sprinting off first to lead the pack. We then all took off running single file behind him up the hill. After a few moments of this military-type regimen, I noticed it symbolically represented a chain of command and I was dead last. I decided this wasn't good enough, so I sped up and passed all the other fighters. I had to show that I belonged. I ran up side by side next to the champ, Jimmy Thunder, my idol. I stayed with him the whole way. Even when he tried to speed up and lose me, I stayed right there with him like a maggot in a dog turd. I wasn't going to leave this camp like a beaten dog with his tail between his legs. I was going to show my fighting heart and courage. The run was long and painful, but I didn't give up and I kept the fast and agonizing pace. At the final stretch, I decided to race past him and beat him in the last remaining hundred yards.

As everyone now finished the run, they all just stared angrily at me. They couldn't believe I had the stamina and will to finish that run on my first try, let alone beat everyone. The jokes then picked up even more, with intimidating comments like, "Yeah, but let's see how he does when he gets his chin hit." I decided to remain calm and quiet to conserve my anger and energy. I knew I was going to be needing both. The only one that didn't say anything was Thunder. He acted like he wasn't affected by me beating him in the run. His quietness rattled me a little for the rest of the drive back to the training camp.

When we got back to the house we all went to our separate quarters to shower and change. We had to first re-energize with a healthy breakfast and then catch a two-hour nap before the real training began. When we sat at the breakfast table, nobody said a word. There was this uneasy silence. It was very unsettling, so I retired early to my room to catch up on some much-needed rest before I had to go train with them.

As I laid in my bed, I heard a few wisecracks and laughter echo from the kitchen. "Hey, coach! Let me get into that virgin ass today! Come on, coach!" I began to shut my eyes and just listen as Rocky's voice kept playing in the back of my mind. "You got this, son, make me proud." I felt his presence. I felt at ease, and surprisingly I drifted off to sleep peacefully.

A couple of hours went by quickly, and then there was a knock at my door. "Let's go make those donuts, son!" I woke up out of my deep slumber in shock once again and rushed to put on my gym gear. As I walked out of my room I braved to ask the question, "What do you mean, make donuts, sir?" At that point everyone started laughing again, their faces engulfed in their hands with disbelief. The coach replied. "You're gonna get your black eyes today, your donuts." The feeling of panic and adrenaline shot through my veins. Oh shit. I'm in for it today, I began thinking. The jokes continued as we all hopped into the same rugged van and began the nerve-wracking venture to the boxing gym.

It was a condemned bowling alley downtown that Big Jon had conveniently turned into a boxing gym. When you walked into the building, your eyes were immediately caught by the four huge, weathered, professional-quality, heavy leather bags that hung silently down from the rafters. As you peered further into the distance, you could see a lonely, rugged, war-torn ring set up in the middle of the bowling lanes. It looked like no gym I had ever seen before, but I knew I was in no place to ask questions, so I kept all my thoughts and remarks to myself.

As I surgically wrapped my hands, the trainer came over and said, "Warm up a bit, then get in the ring. You're sparring

four rounds today. I wanna see what kind of heart we're dealing with here." Another shot of adrenaline coursed through
my being, so I nodded my head and did a light warmup. I
knew I would be needing to conserve my energy if I was going
to last four rounds with any one of these guys.

As one of the more seasoned heavyweights got geared
up next to me, he looked over his shoulder at me, dead in the
eyes, and said, "I'm fuckin' that good ass today, boy." I stood,
paralyzed, with no response or comeback for that comment. I
decided it was better to say nothing, so I just went to the opposite corner and punched the air as I waited for the bell. The coach
unplugged the clock so he could continue putting on his fighter's
gear without distractions. He finished smearing Vaseline all over
the heavyweight's nose, eyes, and mouth and then signaled one
of the other fighters to plug the bell back in. It rang immediately. We didn't even touch gloves in good sportsmanship—he
just came out hard and fast, wasting no time. He had a much
different pace than the amateurs I was used to fighting. I couldn't
time him correctly. He kept moving his head up and down and
side to side while popping me with hard, bell-ringing shots. My
face began to swell and sting while the vibrations of his punches
resonated throughout my body like it was a tuning fork. After a
couple of minutes of this shit, I knew I had to use the one thing
that set me apart from every other living fighter: my incredible
speed and mule-kicking power. So, I decided to tuck my chin
down and just let my hands go while pressing forward.

It worked. I fucked up his expectations with this minor
adjustment. He couldn't keep me off him and soon I was connecting the solid, crisp shots I was known for. I sensed the
whole gym was in shock as this young boy beat the shit out
of one of their seasoned veterans. After a couple of rounds
of this grueling pace, the home run came. I made solid con-

tact and dropped him right on his ass. He fell to the ground and began searching for his mouthpiece. It looked like when Tyson got knocked out by Buster Douglas. He was unconscious, yet somehow still struggling on the mat in desperation. I looked down at him and muttered, "Looks like I got in that ass instead." The coach stepped in the ring and signaled me out. He pointed over to the bag and told me to finish the rest of the round hitting it.

I climbed out of the ropes and walked down the steps of the ring with newfound confidence. All the professionals in the gym came up, patted me on the back, and fist-bumped my boxing gloves. I knew I had just earned my right to be there. The feeling started to creep in that I was the baddest motherfucker in that place. A sense of awesomeness crept into every molecule of my being and my arrogance began to grow.

After weeks of being in the training camp, many times they limited my sparring because I was hurting the other fighters. They would put me in the ring for two or three rounds and then take me out right about the time I began hurting the other fighter, or when he started showing signs of serious distress. I would get taken out and then they'd signal for me to release the rest of my built-up vengeance and anger on the heavy bag. I felt more and more ferocious every day, like an atomic bomb waiting to go off. I even got the long-awaited respect I was looking for from Jimmy Thunder. I never got the chance to spar him, but he would nod and give me a wink of approval occasionally.

Soon, Jon decided to approach me with a professional boxing contract. I was only eighteen, not yet full-grown for a heavyweight. I was 6'3 and 220 pounds at most, but I was extremely fast and strong, and I possessed an exciting style. He must have presented me with a new and revised contract every week, but I would politely decline his offer. I just did not feel ready to jump into the professional circuit at such a young age. I tried to explain this to him, but he refused to listen.

Finally, after months of annoyance and aggravation, I told him I had no choice but to leave because I didn't like the immense pressure he was putting on me. I knew the talent I possessed and I knew I couldn't sell out to just anyone. I was a promoter's wet dream and I needed to be handled correctly. I needed to explore my options and I believed selling out too fast would be moronic. I finally sat down with him and told him that I wanted to go home. I wanted to see my family while I thought things out for what was best for my life and career. I needed some time away without any harassment to make my decision. After hours of failed persuasion, he reluctantly agreed with my decision.

On the way down the mountain, I discovered within myself a new man. I went back home with a new sense of conviction, strength, and confidence in the real gold I now possessed. I was a marketer's hard-on, a boxing promoter's fairytale fantasy. I had the whole fucking package and I needed to be smart. I knew what I had, but I needed to find the right people. To make this dream come true, I needed smart, careful people to get me to the top.

After spending a few weeks in El Paso, I got a phone call from Big Jon. The conversation went on for a couple hours, but at the end of our discussion he finally convinced me to at least try out a trainer in the area that he was very close to. That trainer also lived in New Mexico. The town he lived in was a quick thirty-minute drive from my parents' house. Big Jon told me to at least go see this mythical trainer, that he was a well-kept secret and a genius in the boxing business. He gave me his name and number and urged me again to please make my way out to see him. I knew that I had to keep up my training, and for that I needed a *real* trainer—no amateur coaches in El Paso would suffice. If this guy was as good as Jon said he was, then I should be in really good hands. So I didn't hesitate. I made the phone call that changed my life forever.

CHAPTER 15

MY FIRST TASTE OF HUMBLE PIE

After not wasting too much time being idle, I decided to give this legendary and mysterious trainer a phone call. The first couple of days, I must have called him twenty times with no answer. I would leave a long and detailed message, but in spite of my unfailing effort, there was no return phone call. After a week or so, he finally called me back. We talked for a little while and he seemed indifferent and disinterested. He seemed like a very reluctant man who had been officially "turned off" by the cards the sport of boxing had dealt him. He was actually a good lightweight contender back in the mid 1980s and made quite a name for himself among the people in his hometown. He had tasted glory, but saw the ugly side of the sport as well. That dissonance seemed to resonate in his voice over our phone call. He admitted that he had seen me box a few times before, but that I needed a lot of polishing. I was offended and intrigued by his criticism. He finally agreed to take a look at me and get a sense for my style. So we decided that I could take the quick trip to the gym the next day and meet this myth of a trainer.

I met him at a local city-funded boxing gym off a desolate road in New Mexico. As I waited in the parking lot, counting the tumbleweeds that blew across my fender, I kept staring at the grand warehouse that housed the boxing gym. I couldn't wait to get out and show this man he was dead wrong about everything he thought of me. As I was waiting for his grand arrival, I sat and listened to music, nervously anticipating my future. I sat wondering what kind of stature this mysterious trainer would have. He sounded very witty, charismatic, and tough over the telephone, but you never know how someone will look in person.

As a dumpy white pickup truck rolled up and parked next to me, I looked in my rear-view mirror and saw a short, round-bellied little man hop out of it. He had pale white skin and looked completely out of shape for once having been a world-renowned contender. In my mind, all I could think was that maybe this was the gym janitor or plumber—or that maybe this actually was the mythical trainer, but that he had decided to start living the good life with a steady diet of cheeseburgers and french fries.

I got out of my car and looked over at him. "Are you the guy I talked to on the phone? Are you the guy they call Napoleon?"

He nodded at me and said, "Yup, I sure am. Come on in to the gym and let's see what we can do with you."

From the second I started working out he was impressed with my power and speed, but I also noticed a jigsawed look upon his face. I could tell he liked what he saw, but he thought that I needed some severe tuning. I began loosening up with my relentless movement and started listening to the seeds of instruction he was giving me.

I couldn't believe the knowledge Napoleon had. It was incredible. He was an encyclopedia of boxing technique. We worked hard together that day and we both ended the session satisfied and completely drenched in sweat. I couldn't believe the new science he was teaching me. He was showing me things like angles, slipping, relaxing while punching, etc., and all of this on our very first day!

After a few weeks of me driving back and forth to New Mexico for training, he asked me to move into his country house in order to train harder, with a sense of better focus at hand. After all, I was wasting tons of my money on gas coming from El Paso every day, so I figured it was a logical and great idea. A few short days later, I went ahead and moved in with Napoleon.

He had a beautiful home out by the pecan orchards, with tons of land and good dirt trails for running by the irrigation canals. Once I moved in, we wasted no time at all getting to work. We woke up and ran every single morning and then finished with a hard training regime at dusk. I was severely exhausted every day, and the only rest I would get was at night, while taking short naps in between my hard and lengthy workouts. I had no time for a social life and my schedule would make the boot camp of the military look easy. I was training like a true hardened professional prizefighter. We started to form a bond and he was really starting to feel like a brother and close friend. I lived in the back room of his house and enjoyed studying all of his old fight tapes. He had nostalgic and valuable memorabilia. There were photo albums of legendary fighters, old VHS tapes of all his fights, and vintage fight posters. I thought they were some of the coolest collectables I'd ever seen.

After a few months of consistent training, the Texas Golden Gloves was fast approaching. Napoleon told me, "Let's go win this tournament and then go win nationals, where we can score a big contract." I agreed and began to train every day, diligently and with discipline. We had a continuous routine that we never broke from. I was training like a real fighter now and absorbing everything he was teaching me like an expanding sponge. We would spar all the local heavyweights and light heavyweights in that surrounding area and knock each one out, one after another. There was no stopping me. I was becoming a perfectly trained killer, and now my trainer was grooming me to be the next Heavyweight Champion of the World. We both had no doubt about that, and no one that ever watched me spar or train doubted it either.

Finally it was time for the Golden Gloves, my first real test and proving ground. Napoleon had trained me very hard and we both were ready. On the sign-up day, we learned that my division was jam-packed with talented and experienced contestants. There were heavyweights from the Fort Bliss military, local El Paso heavyweights, and a few Juárez heavyweights who were all wanting to win the Golden Gloves that year. Everyone had ambitions of going to state and then winning big in nationals. Everyone that entered had the same big dream as me. But one thing separated me from the rest—I was the most talented and I knew I worked the hardest of anyone there.

As they drew names for the first night, I was one of the lucky ones to be drawn, along with a kid named Memo. Memo was last year's big winner and he was one mean, tough, brutally strong-willed Mexican heavyweight brawler, with a heavy punch. He weighed close to 300 pounds of hard lard. He was built like a juggernaut, with a big belly, huge shoulders, and thick legs. His head was carved into his shoulders and he looked like a war tank. When the night came for me to climb into the ring, I was nervous at just the look of him. He was all business and I was the skinny kid who barely qualified for the heavyweight division. I weighed in at just one pound over the cruiserweight limit of 200 pounds. I was a lanky 6'4 and resembled a baby giraffe.

We both climbed into the ring to the sound of applause and cheers echoing throughout the convention center. It was a brightly-lit facility and very professionally organized. The Golden Gloves was a major yearly event for die-hard El Paso boxing fans.

Before the first round began, the referee brought us to the center of the ring for our instruction. As we stared at each other, he grinned really wide to show me his mouthpiece. It said FUCK YOU in black marker over the top of it. I gazed at it and slowly turned around to walk back to my corner, wide-eyed and scared to death. Once again, I felt the feeling of fear sweep over me. Napoleon whispered in my ear some kind of constructive instruction, but I couldn't hear anything. Quiet and calm overtook my soul. I focused on my old mentor Rocky. I heard his voice say, "Don't let me down, kid. Go get him, champ." I turned around right when the bell was about to ring with a new sense of strength and vigor. I wasn't scared any more. I was ready and willing to knock this fucker's mouthpiece right out of his Neanderthal-looking skull.

The bell rang. We met each other like two pit bulls in the center. We both traded devastatingly ill-intentioned punches for the first few seconds. I landed my punches cleanly, he didn't. He collapsed headfirst from a vicious left hook I launched at his nasal cavity. He rolled around on the canvas screaming in pain, spitting out his mouthpiece—exactly how I envisioned my success in the few seconds before the bell.

He was counted out in less than one minute of the first round. I walked up to him while he was on the floor and kicked over his mouthpiece while smiling at him and said, "Excuse me, but fuck you."

Napoleon tried to run and pick me up in celebration, but he was too short, so instead we gave each other high-fives and hugged. We climbed out of the ring and tried to leave the building, but people started swarming me for my autograph. It was an experience I wasn't used to and it went immediately to my head like a hot air balloon. All I wanted was a cold beer in celebration and maybe a fine-looking young girl to take home. Little did I know that I was scheduled for another fight the very next night. I was assuming that I had a bye or a pass for the next night. After reflecting on how bad I beat the state favorite, I felt invincible. Nobody left could beat me or even have a remote chance in succeeding against what I was bringing to the boxing world. So after a couple beers, I arrogantly decided to go visit my favorite stomping grounds in the city of Juárez, Mexico and party it up with all my drinking buddies.

In my inexperienced mind, I had just made quick work out of the veteran favorite and there was no competition left even close to my level that could deal my power or speed. I was going to go through this tournament like a hot knife through butter. That night I stayed out until 4 A.M. while my head grew an extra fifty sizes in arrogance and confidence. I thought to myself, this boxing game is really easy for me; I can drink and do whatever the fuck I want to, and nobody is going to beat me. When I finally got home, I went straight to bed so I could sleep the whole rest of the day and night to be refreshed for the next day, when I would have to fight.

That day will forever live on as one of the sorriest, but most valuable, lessons of my whole boxing career. I slept most of the morning and into the day and woke up around 2 P.M. with an extreme headache and hangover with the urgent need to urinate. As I uncoordinatedly lumbered into my bathroom,

I heard the my parents' house phone ring and ring and ring. I ignored it at first, but it wouldn't stop. It sounded like an emergency. I wasn't going to answer it, but the hangover was killing me.

I answered the phone. It was Napoleon on the other end, yelling, "Where the fuck have you been?"

I said, "What do you mean?"

He said, "You're picked to fight again today, man! Let's get moving! We have to be there by 4 P.M. to report and start warming up!" I hung up the phone immediately and felt my knees get wobbly and weak. I had royally screwed up and I started thinking of excuses to pull out of the fight. I was so hung over I couldn't even see the oven clock in front of me, and I had to be ready to fight in two hours. I pounded a gallon of water and grabbed my gear, robe, and trunks, then sped off to the civic center.

I raced into the parking structure, got out of my car, and signed some more autographs while making my way up the stairs to my dressing room. I was late. Extremely late. Napoleon just looked at me and said, "I don't even want to know what the fuck you were doing and I want no excuses. You gotta get your ass in the ring in fifteen minutes."

That left us with enough time to wrap my hands, but no time to warm up. He quickly wrapped my hands, slid on my headgear, and tied my boxing gloves. On our way into the ring from the dressing room, he kept yelling in my ear, "Focus, goddammit! Focus!"

All I could hear was the loud music of the night before and all I could taste was the liquor marinating in my dry mouth. Next thing I knew, I was in the center of the ring for instruction. After going back to my corner to hug Napoleon and begin the fight, the fight was already over, except I was in a fog and it was the other guy jumping up and down in celebration. I was confused and wondering if the bell had even rung yet. Why was he jumping up and down?

I stumbled back to my corner, senseless and disoriented. I even sat on my corner stool backwards. I looked up and noticed that Napoleon had a disappointed and angered look spread all across his face. He began pouring water all over my head to try and bring me back to my senses. The realization began to set in that I literally had just gotten knocked the fuck out. I could sense all my dreams fade away like a vapor. This time, everything I worked so hard for went with it. My years of built-up confidence, my deceptive and false arrogance, and now my dreams and inspiration were all gone. I was once again destroyed, emotionally and mentally. I realized it would be a long and treacherous road back to redemption.

CHAPTER 16

BREAKING THE PATTERN

I wanted to just curl up in the fetal position and die. I had failed my dream and I had failed Rocky. I was careless and my worst nightmare had come true: I wasn't the talented badass I thought I was. I lost the Golden Gloves at a regional level. This was inexcusable and I knew I wasn't championship material. The only punishment I could inflict on myself for being such a failure was what I'd always done in times of distress: I would hit the bars and nightlife with my drinking friends again. But first I needed to get my belongings out of Napoleon's house. I needed to get over there and clean out my room so I could head back home with my tail between my legs, like I'd always done. When I pulled up to his home, I noticed the front door was slightly open.

As I approached the door and walked into his house, there was an eerie stillness that resonated throughout the whole house. All I could hear was the sound of water dripping slowly from the bathroom faucet next to my bedroom. As I quietly walked into the room to secretly grab and pack up my belongings, my gaze fell on the dresser mirror. It had an *El Paso*

Times article cut out and taped to it. The date just so happened to be from that day's paper, and it was fresh off the press. I noticed my picture so I slowly walked up and read it. As I read the article, I stood in silence. It was a one-sided article that was bashing my performance and celebrating my upset while giving glory to the kid that had had zero chance in beating me. His name was Carlos Tapia and was a sound, solid and brave boxer to whom I still give much credit to this very day. He capitalized on my careless weakness and found his day of glory.

As I continued to read, I stood in stillness and grief. I could literally hear my faint and shallow breathing, along with the echoing sounds of the slow, repetitive droplets of water coming out of the bathroom faucet. As if I couldn't feel any lower, Napoleon made sure it was his job that I did. As I stood there staring in shock at the article, I heard his voice from the doorway entrance. He said, "You can't go out like this, you gotta prove everybody wrong. I hope you make the right decision." I stared blankly at the article for a few more seconds and then turned around and looked at Napoleon with a sense of hatred. It was at that very moment I heard that familiar voice of tough love, but this time it wasn't from my father or Rocky. Napoleon had suspected what my behavior had been the night before the fight and knew it was a serious lesson that I had to learn on my own. He saw my careless arrogance and my false confidence. He knew the serious talent that I possessed and he knew what I would be wasting if I ran away, like I had always done. My pattern had always been to let my demons pull me into the darkness of hell whenever I felt any kind of failure.

I glanced back at the article and then back at him. "Why would you try and make me feel worse about this?" He stared right back at me and shrugged his shoulders. "You can't keep running, Dave." I watched him turn around and walk down the hallway.

I knew exactly what he meant. I knew I had to do what was toughest in my mind, and face my humility like a man of strength and character. I couldn't run anymore, not only because it was cowardly but because it was exhausting. It was time for me to grow into a man and face down my demons.

I just dropped my head in grief and laid down the article. I slumped down on the edge of the bed, put my hands over my face, and let out a long weeping sigh for what l knew would be the longest and toughest round of life ahead. I sat for a long while in privacy, contemplating all the obstacles I would now have to overcome. The task that once seemed so promising now looked bleak, grim and daunting.

Half an hour later, Napoleon walked back to the bedroom door and said, "Gym tomorrow. Get some rest." I now slumped completely back down on the bed and let out a painful, grief-stricken yell. I knew now that what was good for me wasn't always going to be what felt good. I realized that what makes a champion is what you do while your mind and body is in pain, and doing what's right despite having these feelings.

The next day, we did just that. I woke up for my morning run over the irrigation canals, instead of running from the Mexican police, drunk and belligerent. I knew the humility and pain was going to be a part of my lesson, and I decided to adopt a mature and spiritual view of what I deemed my failure. I decided to take the golden nugget of experience away from it and see it as a valuable lesson from God.

Napoleon and I worked hard and continuously throughout the next few months, and ended up entering some smaller amateur shows around the New Mexico and Arizona area. Once again, I won all those amateur fights by knockout, but I still couldn't shake the horrific and tragic loss that had ruined my chances for greatness. It ate at my conscience and soul every day. I knew I had to accept it, or it would fester inside my guts for the rest of my life.

I decided the only wise thing to do was to swallow the big spoonful of humble pie and use it as my teacher, something I could reflect upon in the battles ahead. It is what would propel me to ignite the bright and promising professional boxing career on which I was about to embark.

CHAPTER 17

THE JOURNEY BEGINS

The time had finally arrived. We had sat down and had a serious and truthful discussion, and we felt the time was now. A couple of grueling years after my initial loss in the Golden Gloves, amateur fighting for plastic trophies felt useless to our goal now. We had figured we had enough experience with my short life in the amateurs, and having more fights would only serve us better in the professional world circuit. Napoleon felt that our work had now matured to the professional level where we wanted it to be, and we were now ready for blastoff.

After much thought on who would manage me, Napoleon decided to go through his huge, archaic Rolodex of managers' numbers for weeks on end. He had me interview with all the old 80s and 90s managers he had known and trusted over the years. I spoke to each one over the phone, not really getting a good instinct or vibe off of any one of them. They all seemed to be in too quick of a hurry to make a quick buck. I knew this was the flesh-peddling business and that to many of these wolves I was the damsel in distress.

We must have talked to at least a dozen prospects before we finally came across our guy. I was on my way to Austin that weekend and I was planning to stop and say hello to an old high school friend in Dallas on the way. I told Napoleon about my plans and he said, "Dallas? Wait. Oh man! I know just the guy for us!" I looked at him a little puzzled and wondered who the hell he could be talking about.

He ran over to his Rolodex and began combing through his set of vintage numbers once more. I heard him call a few boxing people for leads to this mystery man's number. After no more than ten minutes, he was talking to the man himself. I had to wait patiently while I heard them play catch-up for at least a good half-hour, but then it was all down to business.

After reminiscing with one boxing story after another, Napoleon handed me the phone and said, "Introduce yourself, this is our man." I picked up the phone and without hesitation I introduced myself. I'll never forget the first time hearing his voice over the phone. Marlon Brando had nothing on this guy. He was Italian and he had the deepest voice I had ever heard come from a man. I pictured a fat, hairy man with gold rings on each of his fingers, puffing on a Cuban cigar. He sounded completely mobster, and I felt a bit hesitant. His alias in this book will be Salami Slammer.

After speaking with him for a good half hour, I started to ease into the conversation a bit. He became less threatening after he laughed a few times and made some casual jokes about the brutality of the boxing business. I told him I was going to be heading to Austin for the ACL music festival, but would be swinging by Dallas to say hello to a buddy. He sounded pleased and told me to stop in and get a good workout at Gary's Street Boxing Gym, located in the downtown district of Dallas.

I responded, "Not a problem, sir. I'll definitely be there to check it out and show you what I'm made of!"

I must admit, I hung up extremely nervous, but excited about the future and what it might hold. Things were finally beginning to feel right again. I wasn't about to let this opportunity pass me by and I was definitely ready to prove I was ready for the next level. Salami knew the business; he had handled many contenders and world champions. He was known as a great but careful handler in the boxing world—exactly the type of guy I wanted running the future of my career.

After a few days had passed, I began packing my things. Napoleon came into my room and informed me to pack for at least a month. He told me that he wanted me to train out there for a while and get a feel for their routine and schedule. He wanted them to get to know me, and vice versa. I really didn't have anything else going on, so I obliged with an excited grin from ear to ear. But I had one question. "Hey Napoleon, where exactly am I going to be staying?" He replied, "Oh, don't you worry about that. Salami promised a nice spot for you when you get there." I thought, this is going to be great, I can just feel it. In excitement, I impulsively decided that I couldn't wait any longer and that I had to leave the next day.

I said goodbye to my parents before embarking on my life's journey. I was on my way to follow my dream; I was embarking on the start of what would be the beginning of a bright and colorful boxing career. Hours into the drive, I decided to go ahead and skip Austin and take the full drive to Dallas. I was too excited to get started on my life as a fighter. The entire drive to Dallas was a good thirteen hours of Red Bull and caffeine pills. I was a bundle of nerves the whole drive, high as a kite, so I didn't nod off and fall asleep. I kept contact with Salami on my new cell phone and would give him my e.t.a. every couple of hours.

As I got closer and began getting into the Dallas city limits, I got my first real taste of the congested traffic. It was Dallas traffic at its finest. I was stuck in construction and traffic, trying to find this gym without any of the luxuries we take for granted today, like GPS. I had nothing to guide me but the detailed instructions that I wrote on a chocolate-covered napkin from Dunkin Donuts. Getting into Dallas took me at least another three hours or more.

As I finally got to the downtown exit, it was now getting very late. It had to be at least 11 P.M. I was now in the vicinity of the gym and I knew they were still up waiting for me. They still had to give me a proper introduction and settle me into my hotel. I was now driving through the area where the gym was located, looking at all the homeless people and the badly addicted drug users on skid row. It was a bad area, and especially so at night. After aimlessly driving around the downtown area with Salami patiently directing me with one turn after another, I finally made it.

As my luck would have it, my bucket of rolling bolts got a flat tire at precisely the exact moment I hit the gym parking lot. I was extremely exhausted and things were not living up to my expectations. I had a flat tire in the middle of the downtown Dallas homeless area at 11 P.M., when the crack heads were out strolling around for their next fix like a bunch of bloodthirsty zombies. I stepped out of my car, bug-eyed, while still seeing tracers from the horrendous drive. All I wanted was a hot shower and a home-cooked meal. I walked up to the entrance and banged on the gym door as I swayed back and forth in fatigue.

I could barely see through the glass, so I cuffed my hands together and began peering inside. I saw a silhouette of an extremely skinny, unimpressive, funny-looking man hopping down the stairs with an obnoxious grin. He was wearing white sneakers, rolled-up jeans, and a black long-sleeved shirt with the sleeves rolled up as well. He opened the door and just smiled at me. Startled, I stepped back a bit and figured this had to be the janitor who had the graveyard shift at the gym that night. As we looked each other over for a moment, I analyzed his rugged-looking face. He had sunken cheeks that followed the curvature of his exaggerated cheek bones, a crooked yet pointy nose with bushels of long black hair coming out of both nostrils, gigantic black hairy eyebrows, and a full head of brown messy hair. He looked to be about in his early fifties.

After gazing at me for a few moments in what looked like satisfaction, he opened his mouth and began to speak. I stumbled back a few steps and almost dropped my things. This was the same voice I heard on the phone? His deep, rugged voice definitely did not match his frame, face, or stature.

I shook his hand in shock and muttered, "Hey, listen, I'm extremely tired and I need to take a shower and get some food. I also just got a flat tire rolling into this place."

He looked at my car and then looked back at me. "Well, the best we can do is have you stay here at the gym tonight in the back room."

I thought that this guy had lost his fucking mind. "Are you being serious? I'm tired, man. I have to work out tomorrow and I need good rest." He looked up at me and I could tell he did not give one shit about what I had to say. He pointed to the door and told me to grab my things and come in. As I made my way inside, I noticed the leaky roof with multiple annoying drips, a grungy, torn-up blue carpet and the smell of dingy, worn-out leather from the beaten gym bags. I noticed the huge, Texas-sized roaches that would scatter across the walls and floor every time he showed me into another room.

This crazy man expected me to stay here? I thought I was turning pro and would be put up at the Ritz-Carlton or something similarly lavish—except this was the fight business, and those rules don't apply for this sport. They want a fighter that's hungry and determined, not a spoiled little brat with a silver spoon in his mouth and a taste for caviar and Beaujolais. They wanted Spartans hungry for war, not pampered athletes with multimillion-dollar signing bonuses but no heart. This was only the beginning of proving myself and I was not going to back down from any challenge. I would gladly accept the test and I would win at any cost. If this is how I would be tested, so be it. When he escorted me to the back room, there was already a fighter sleeping in there. All that was left was a grimy, sweat-stained couch in the far corner. Salami threw me a pillow and blanket, telling me he would see me first thing in the morning.

I knew I wanted the hell out of there. I decided I couldn't take it, and was formulating my escape before it dawned on my tired mind that I had a flat tire with no spare. I was stuck in that shithole for the rest of the night. As I laid down on the couch, I folded my arms behind my head. I was trying to fall asleep, but my cellmate snored too loudly and farted in his sleep. It was also in the middle of the summer humidity and there was no air conditioning. The room was stuffy and extremely hot. My tired, baggy eyes watched the hours count down until the dreaded morning.

When the short hand of the clock touched the five, the gym boxing bell began ringing like a broken alarm clock with no snooze button. I could hear a loud commotion from multiple people inside the gym area. Then a loud blast of gospel music started blaring throughout the whole gym. It sounded like whoever was in there was staging a church revival. As I made my way to the gym area, I peeked in and saw a team of nicely outfitted, athletic black people holding hands and bowing their heads in prayer. All of them had brightly-colored red and black track suits on, with white laced-up boxing shoes. A few resembled coaches and were taking the necessary gear out of their bags to start a workout.

In that moment of confusion I started to glance around the room and see if I could recognize anybody. I couldn't believe my eyes. I was in the presence of greatness. It was the man himself. It was Evander "The Real Deal" Holyfield. The reigning Heavyweight Champion of the World. I stared in disbelief and immediately all the exhaustion overrunning my body was gone. I was about to get a front row seat to watch Evander Holyfield train. They were gearing up for some of the most intense and exciting sparring I had ever seen.

As I grabbed a chair and sat back in the corner, I tried to calm my excitement. I watched in awe for a full two hours as Evander Holyfield trained and sparred like a gladiator preparing for war. I'll never forget the sound of the leather cracking as the punches landed one after the other. It sounded painfully brutal, but I was extremely impressed at his finesse and grace in the ring. He made a grueling and brutal sport look like a beautiful and elegant dance fit for a ballerina. After his sparring, I got to watch him work on his technique with the heavy bag. He trained like a purebred fighting pit bull. I had never seen such a disciplined work ethic in all of my life. That was exactly where I wanted to be. I knew this was exactly the gym I wanted to be in, despite its discomfort.

CHAPTER 18

THE DEAL WITH THE DEVIL

It was only hours later, after Evander finished up his workout, that the other professionals poured inside. The gym instantly turned into a madhouse, filled with good, seasoned veteran professionals. This was no white-collar gym. Business folk and weekend warriors were not welcome. This gym was dedicated to the most serious professional boxers only. It could be compared to the likes of an Olympic training center for gymnasts, except this facility was for professional boxers.

I paced around the gym nervously, wondering who the hell Salami could have gotten me for a trainer. I knew that, like all hard-nosed boxing trainers, he was going to want to test me, and probably would have me sparring that same day. Trainers like to see what they have before they start putting their dedication and time into a fighter. They want to see the skill, heart, and determination of a fighter before they decide to start training him. The main ingredient they look for is how well you respond under adversity and fire. "Fire" is the term they use to see if you can actually fight when you're exhausted or badly hurt. During the mid to late rounds of a fight, fatigue and the accumulation of punches start to sink into the body and mind of a fighter. You either fold up and crumble to the canvas, or you pull the championship greatness out from your soul. That is the main ingredient they look for before deciding to go any further with a pupil.

After the hours counted down, the gym door swung wide open and in came a short, wobbling old black man, carrying an oversized gym bag. He reminded me of a black Danny DeVito. He yelled, loudly, "Where's my new fighter at? Who knows where to find this big great white heavyweight that supposedly punches like a mule!" I knew he was talking about me so I sheepishly grinned, stuck out my hand and walked toward him for a proper introduction.

As I walked up to him with my hand extended he looked me up and down and said, "Watcha tryin to do, boy? I ain't got no time for dat! Get yo big goofy ass up in dat ring and start movin around a little fo me boy! I wanna take a look at what I've got to work wit." I knew he had seen his fair share of potential prospects come in and out of that gym over the years, but I was confident that once he saw me, he was going to be pleased with excitement. I climbed into the ring, already wrapped up, and began my routine of shadowboxing.

I'll never forget the look on his face. His exact words were, "Sweet Jesus, will you look at this shit. I ain't neva in my life seen a white boy move like this."

I said, "I'm not really white, sir, I'm half Mexican."

He said, "You white, son. I don't categorize the shades of white on the color spectrum."

I said, "Yeah, I know, but in all honesty..."

"Shut up and work, son! Ain't nobody tell you you can be askin me any questions round here! Here we work!"

I just nodded in agreement. I thought for sure that this

motherfucker was crazy. I didn't even know his name. I was feeling very reluctant, but I decided to ask him, even though the consequences of this question might piss him off. "Excuse me sir, but I never caught your name?" He replied, "That's because I didn't give it, you stupid shit. It's Potato Pie, now get back to work!" At that point, I was fueling with anger and didn't even want to ask him how he got that ridiculous name.

After a good eight rounds of shadowboxing in the humid heat, I was drenched in sweat and filled with exhaustion. I wasn't used to this type of humid heat and there was no ventilation inside the boxing gym. After I thought the workout was over, I leaned over the ropes to catch my breath. After no more than a few moments, I noticed these two huge muscular black fighters swagger into the gym. They stood about 6'6 and 6'4 and each weighed approximately 270 pounds. They were very large, intimidating-looking men. They said hello to Potato Pie and told him they were there to spar with Holyfield, but they got into town just the day before so they wanted to come in to try and get in some good work. Potato Pie turned and pointed at me and said, "There's your Holyfield right there." I looked at him wide-eyed, like he was fucking crazy. I wanted to run over to him and shove him off the side of the ring for saying such a ridiculous and stupid comment that could get me killed. The two fighters looked at me and said, "Okay, we gonna go get gloved up. Let's get to work."

Once again I felt a streak of fear come over me. I mean, holy shit, these guys were monsters and they were probably going to dismantle and destroy my white ass. Potato Pie walked over to me and began to slide the worn-out leather headgear over my head while putting Vaseline all over my nose, lips, and eyes. He whispered, "Okay, these guys are ringers, son. I want you to work the jab and not get too cute. Box like you know how to box. If they hurt you with a good shot, give it back to 'em and earn your respect. Remember, work the jab and throw your punches when you see the openings."

Once again I was standing there, scared out of my confused, bewildered and now exhausted mind. I began loosening up as the first huge mountain of a man climbed into the center of the ring. In my mind, he *was* the ring. There was nowhere to go. He was showing his presence by stretching and blowing snot out of his nose as he made loud groans and yells. It was like some kind of intimidation warrior call. He wanted me to know that he owned that square space and he meant nothing but business. Potato Pie put the finishing touches of Vaseline on his face as well, then yelled out, "Next bell!" That meant we had a little under thirty seconds before it was go time. That thirty seconds came and went like a mid summer breeze. After one last slug of the water bottle, the bell gave a loud ring and Pie yelled, "Work time fellas!"

I decided to go right at him throwing fast and piercing jabs, but I was missing. I felt lethargic and exhausted from the previous eight rounds of shadowboxing. I was hitting nothing but air and his wide muscular shoulders. The next thing I knew was a WHACK and a BOOM! He landed two huge shots on me that almost knocked me out. I was holding on to him for dear life as he kept punching my ribs and face. Every punch was extremely hard and they were hurting me badly. I had a funny smell of iron in my nose and everything was getting blurry. I was beginning to get that familiar feeling of being in the Golden Gloves after the knockout. I knew I was still standing, but knocked out on my feet—I just hadn't gone down yet. He was extremely strong and kept coming forward like a bulldozer with vicious punches. BING, BANG, BING is all I could hear as my head rang like a tuning fork. I was literally getting destroyed in front of the whole gym. Out of my peripheral vision I could see the crowd that was now circling around the ring. I felt like I was a little kitten fending off a hungry lion. I was hoping for the bell to ring and I was counting down the seconds until my savior gave me the sound of deliverance.

Then I noticed his teeth biting down on his mouthpiece as he tried to finally put me out, and something inside me changed. I got mad. When I get mad, I get mean. I started to believe in myself and began firing back. I wasn't trying to fend him off anymore. I was now trying to kill the son of a bitch. You could hear both our punches land and echo throughout the gym. It turned into an all-out gym war. We kept firing crisp and heavy punches on each other while not giving up an inch on either side. The bell finally rang, except I wasn't done with him just yet. We got a standing ovation of applause from everybody in the gym. I walked back to the corner a changed man. This time, I had the look of a stone cold killer. Potato Pie said, "How you feelin, son?" I said, "Fuckin fabulous. Let's go five more!" For the first time, my opponent looked at me with fear in his eyes. He knew he had just flipped a switch and I had gone Charles Manson fucking insane. He nodded at me in agreement and we touched gloves to start the second bell. We didn't waste any time. We started throwing bombs at each other once again. We traded back and forth for a few seconds, but this time I was ferocious and angry. I started connecting with cleaner shots and I was backing him up for the first time. The next thing I know was BAM! He fell headfirst into the canvas. I dropped his ass. He fell forward onto his chin, lying unconscious with blood coming out of the corners of both his eyes and nose.

He started to roll over and struggle to make his way up when Potato Pie got in the middle of us and yelled, "That's good, son! You fought your heart out, son. Good work."

Pie headed over to the other fighter and started taking off his gear and splashing cold water all over his face. He signaled to me to get out of the ring and go hit the heavy bag. I slowly made my way over to the heavy bag like a lion cub who had just had his first real kill. I was smiling from ear to ear. I had just proved myself in my biggest test yet. The rest of my workout that day went by with confidence and ease. At the end of the workout Potato Pie walked up to me and yelled, "My killa!" I couldn't help but smile even more, because right then I knew I had earned his respect and it felt amazing.

At the end of my workout, I showered and went to the back room where I had slept the night before and just sat there for a few minutes to let it all soak in. I knew it was only a matter of time before a legitimate contract would get presented to me. I was ready, excited and willing to sign anything. I was overcome with emotional tears.

After only a few hours, I got a call on the office phone from the Salami himself. He said, "I'll be down in a couple hours with a contract and an offer for your bonus."

I sat still, holding the phone with disbelief and excitement. My dream was on its way to becoming a reality. After a few hours, he showed up and sat me down. "I heard what you did, that's pretty amazing."

I agreed and nodded frantically up and down with a full smile. As I sat looking at the contract, desperate and amazed, all I wanted to do was sign the damn thing and get going with my dream. He scanned through the contract with me and explained the details of what it meant.

I said, "Well, if I'm not comfortable to sign this, could we at least have a different one drawn up, that could be the final one?"

He looked at me with confidence and consoled me with

a smile. "Absolutely, son, not a problem at all. Let's just sign this one temporarily and get busy on these next few fights. As they get bigger and tougher, we will draw up a brand new one." I nodded my head eagerly in full agreement and inked my signature on the dotted line.

To this day I don't know why I didn't call my father for consultation and let him negotiate for me. I was filled with emotion, wild-eyed, full of promise and ready to conquer the world. I didn't care about all the mindless lingo of some boring business contract. This was the start of an awesome and beautiful boxing career, but not reading the fine print would later catch up to me. I didn't know the type of character I was dealing with. Always be careful of those who can smile to your face while patting you on the back. Sometimes those are the biggest snakes in the grass. After we signed, he hugged me and handed me a bonus check. He said, "Now go get yourself a nice place to stay in Dallas, kiddo."

CHAPTER 19

MY FIRST TASTE OF
GLORY AND GROUPIES

Ring entrance

We got to work immediately. I kept the little amount of money I had brought with me to Dallas and I decided to stay there until I could get my first fight out of the way and break the ice. We called Napoleon and told him I would be fighting by the fall, and that in the meantime I was just going to stay in Dallas to get the correct training and sparring.

I leased myself an apartment in a beautiful and flourishing upscale neighborhood in the Dallas suburban area. It was a good, clean area and my place was actually quite nice, except I had no furniture beyond a beat-up mattress and one of those heavy, square television sets that could only receive basic cable. My limited furniture had been donated by some divorced couple moving out of their apartment a couple doors down. I had placed a framed picture of my family on the top of the television set to remind me of my longing for home, when nothing of interest was on the three lousy basic cable channels my coat hanger for an antenna could pick up. All of these inconveniences would just have to do until I could get my first fight out of the way.

The months of hard, dedicated training rolled by. Before the first scheduled fight, I ended up getting extremely ill, which forced me to decide to reschedule the fight. I personally believe it was due to the overtraining and not having the proper comforts at home to really take care of myself. I really wanted to be home by Christmas, but being sick meant postponing the fight, and that meant I had to train through the holidays and sacrifice being with my family.

My life consisted of the familiar daily routine: waking up to run the four-mile stretch of Katy Trail Park, eat breakfast, fight the horrific traffic to the downtown gym, train hard as hell for three hours, and then go back home to sleep and do it all over again the next day. I had absolutely no life and I had become extremely homesick, especially when I knew all my friends were out having fun partying and traveling. I would sometimes call my parents from the archaic flip phone that I had, in tears of frustration and loneliness. I hated being away from my friends and loved ones, but my dad always had a way of calmly talking courage into me when I was emotionally beaten down. I would always hang up the phone with a newfound strength and desire.

As December drew closer, all I wanted was to fight my fight and hurry back home to celebrate the new year with my first professional win and be around my family. The date couldn't come quickly enough. I had been alone for months on end with no friends or family. I was finally tired of the training and grueling daily routine. My body and mind now badly needed to rest and recharge. I was dealing with exhaustion, boredom, and homesickness.

During that time, Salami Slammer was managing another huge, good-looking heavyweight who was a lot further along in his career than I was. He was a big Middle Eastern guy that stood in the range of 6'5, strong, with a granite chin. He had fought all the top contenders and was already a well-known household boxing name. I looked up to his accomplishments back then. Let's go ahead and call him Frankenstein. He was my main sparring partner every week for months on end. I was only fighting a four-rounder at the time, so sparring with him for three or four rounds a few times a week was part of my training routine. He was actually easy sparring for me, because he was extremely slow. Every time I let my hands go I could hit him six punches to his one, but he could take one helluva hard punch. It was almost as if I missed him; while I was punching, he would get insulted. He was basically a giant, heavy bag with eyeballs.

All he did for his preparation was to spar almost every day. Sometimes he would rotate two to three guys at a time and go a full ten rounds in the gym. This is guaranteed to get you into great shape, but the beatings he took wouldn't be good for any fighter. Sparring every day takes a huge toll on your body and mind. It's been eight years since we trained together, and I've heard that these days you can hardly understand him when he talks; he slurs his speech and mumbles like a newborn baby wanting his bottle.

Frankenstein used to pick me up on sparring days to get

a quick run on Katy Trail, then we'd head straight to the downtown boxing gym. We trained with the same trainer and lived in the same area, so it was convenient. He would try to coach and counsel me during our car ride. He'd tell me about what to expect from the professional boxing world—what to do, what not to do. He told me continuous horror stories, but half of the time I couldn't understand anything he said. It was like listening to a two-year-old make up words to describe something he saw while playing in the sandbox. It was agonizing to listen to him, but I respected his experience.

Please understand that I appreciated the company and friendship of Frankenstein, but it made me realize that I didn't want to end up in his condition after my boxing career. His company was a lesson in and of itself. I knew I wanted to use boxing, not let boxing use me. He was a punch-drunk fighter, still able to function and roam the world, but he was always kind to me and he was Salami's main money generator. I needed to follow his lead to get to the top, and any advice was appreciated, but by watching him I also learned valuable lessons on what *not* to do.

Fight night finally arrived and I was ready. There was one minor problem, though. I didn't have a pair of boxing shorts or a comfortable ride to the venue. Frankenstein came to my aid. He picked me up outside my apartment, smiling as he held up the boxing trunks. As he drove me to the venue, he gave me pointers the whole way there, psyching me up. I listened intensely the whole way to the Dallas Downtown convention center and hotel. The fights were held inside the fancy ballroom and one of the main sponsors was some local titty bar. It was a low-budget production, but the noisy crowd-filled ballroom and cigar smoke gave it the gritty Las Vegas fight feel. Many of Dallas's richest and most successful socialites attended.

I was scheduled for the first fight of the night. I ended up getting there at 4 P.M. but my fight wasn't scheduled until 7:00, which was right when the doors opened. You always had to arrive a few hours early before fights, to register with the commission and get prepared properly. When I arrived I was a nervous wreck, but deep down I was truly confident. I was fighting a guy by the name of Earl Martin. He'd only had about three fights and wasn't very talented. He was a thick-shouldered black man and looked very strong, but I noticed he never made intimidating eye contact with me. He would only look at me with a glance of hesitation and uncertainty. I knew I was going to eat this man alive. My confidence grew. I was feeling like a caged lion and he was going to be my first real taste of a proper kill. As I got warmed up and ready in the dressing room, the moment had finally arrived. My team circled around me and started clapping their hands and continuously chanting, "LET'S GO CHAMP!"

I could feel my confidence grow even more and I was feeling like a million bucks. I was as sharp as a knife and I was mentally ready to kill this man. I was hitting the mitts so hard that it sounded like cracks of lightning echoing throughout the dressing room. I felt absolutely invigorated and amazing. The commissioner came in to tell me it was go time, and everyone formed a single file line with me in the very front. The security guards swung the doors open and we began the slow walk through the dark tunnel into the ring. All I could hear were the screams of the crowd and the loud entrance music blaring. I saw flashes of camera lights in the corners of my eyes and hands reaching out to touch me. It was so much to take in that my breathing became faint. I was floating on weightless legs. Nothing seemed real. It was as if I was in a lucid dream.

I approached the ring and saw the stairs up the entrance.

I took my slow, calculated steps up into the gladiator pit. I felt as if I was climbing up the steps of Mount Olympus and entering into the ring of the Pantheon. The crowd went even more wild. I looked around for a few more seconds to take in my surroundings, the multitudes of people cheering. My eyes caught the spotlight focused on my opponent, walking through the same doors, wearing all black and punching into the air. He walked slowly during his entrance with a look of focus and intensity. He entered the ring and couldn't even look me in the eyes. He was obviously too shook up and scared. We met in the center of the ring and both listened to the referee's brief instruction. We touched gloves and went back to our opposing corners. It was just him and me. Everyone else climbed out of the ring. It was sheer silence as we anticipated the first bell. You could cut the tension with a knife.

I heard my first professional DING DING! I rushed out to meet him in the center of the ring to impose my dominance. He mustered up what bravery he had stored within his soul and threw a few sharp combinations at me, with only one punch slightly connecting upon my temple. I could already feel a difference in the smaller and lighter professional boxing gloves. He grazed my chin with another punch. Starting to feel desperate, I instinctively spun off to my left and cracked him in the liver with a brutal body punch followed by a few devastating strikes landing upstairs to his skull. He stepped back and his eyes widened like he'd just seen Satan himself. There was no time or place for him to hide. I smelled blood and I was ready for the kill. I wasted no time and began my own onslaught of vicious penetrating punches. I charged him relentlessly and ferociously with devastating punches until his back was flat on the canvas. The referee moved in and brushed me out of the way to start the ten count. I sprinted to the neutral corner. As I stood there, out of breath, the referee waved off the fight and took Earl Martin's mouthpiece out of his beaten and bloodied skull. With the sudden feeling of overwhelming excitement, I ran over to my corner and hugged everyone on my team. The referee walked over to my corner and brought me back to the center of the ring and raised my arm in victory. I had finally scored my first win and knockout as a professional fighter, and in only the first round. As I made my way out of the ring, I felt like a living god.

I saw the doctor for the examination process and then I went over to the commissioner to receive my pathetic paycheck. My first-ever check was for $400, but I didn't mind because the experience alone was worth ten million dollars in my mind. As I tried pushing through the hordes of people between me and my dressing room, I decided to stop and sign autographs for the mobs of excited people. This new life that was bestowed upon me was a fantasy come true and it was about to get even better. As I approached my dressing room, I noticed a line of about eight beautiful women just waiting with smiles on their faces in nervous desperation. I asked my friend Danny, "What the fuck do you think this is all about, bro?" He looked at me with confusion and just shrugged his shoulders. As I got into my dressing room to change, I asked him to go outside and see what they wanted or what the commotion was about. He walked out for a few moments and then returned pale as a ghost. "Dude, they basically just want to go party with us and hang out with our crew the rest of the night."

I had no fucking idea where I was going to go party, but I knew Salami Slammer had gotten me a room at that hotel for the night just in case I had decided to celebrate and drink. Out of curiosity, I left my dressing room without a shirt on to speak with the girls. I discovered they were mainly strippers that were just about to get off of work cocktailing for the fights. As I spoke to them, one impulsively grabbed me and licked all the sweat and blood droplets off my chest and then began to kiss me. In shock, I wondered if she didn't know, or didn't care, that the blood on my chest wasn't my own. I gradually pushed her away with an inviting smile and gave them all my room number. I whispered in her ear that I would be there within the next thirty minutes while caressing her hand. Danny and I rushed back into the dressing room and frantically gathered together all my belongings. Danny had the job of supplying the party favors, so he took a cab to the local convenience store and bought cases of alcohol and lambskin condoms. When we met at the hotel room, we let in all eight girls. We turned up the music, poured the alcohol and began partying all night in overjoyed celebration. It was just myself and my best friend, and we had eight beautiful and sexy women to ourselves. At that moment, I knew I was hooked on the groupie lifestyle that boxing had rewarded me with.

I had continuous sex and orgies with different girls the remainder of the night. It was a hungry man's buffet of pussy and it was all mine. The girls were young and beautiful and it just seemed that they all wanted to be around me. It was the strangest and most superficial feeling I have ever had, but I wasn't going to overthink it. I felt like a Roman gladiator being rewarded for his victorious battle with sex and goblets of alcohol. The night didn't just end there—they ended up calling more of their friends and this debauchery went on for another two whole nights. It was sex, sex and even more sex with one beautiful woman after another. I was hooked and there was no way out of this one. I found a new addiction besides fighting and alcohol. It was my new love for groupies, and there were plenty more of them coming. I now knew what the fruits of my labor would bring me, and it was everything I'd ever wanted.

CHAPTER 20

WINNING A CHAMPIONSHIP
WITH DISGUST

First belt

My career was going fast. It had its ups and downs, but overall, I was steamrolling through every opponent with a defined purpose and goal. Every fight had its challenges, but I was wrecking everyone they put in front of me. After passing my tests with nothing but gold stars, I finally got my break at my very first title shot. It was the Texas Heavyweight Championship and I was going to be fighting a tough redneck, backwoods kid named Johnny Connelly. He didn't have anything special except size, toughness and the will to win. I knew I'd be in trouble if I didn't play my cards right. I couldn't make one small mistake with this guy, because he was known to get sloppy and throw wide looping punches over the top of taller fighters. If he hit me on top of the head with one of those crazy wild shots, it could be good night for me. My record was 12-0 with twelve big knockouts. He was 8-1 with six big knockouts, and at the time he was considered a durable test.

Before the fight, I trained in a sparsely populated town in New Mexico with Napoleon. We had an agreement with Salami to bring us some tough and durable sparring a month before the fight. I sparred with fighters that fit Connelly's style and which were considered even better than him. Doing this type of training builds your confidence and toughens your game plan. We trained hard and consistently for three months, and the last month was always the time I would get sharp with the hard, rugged sparring. After the first two months of breaking my body completely down, the sparring would be absolutely grueling.

Whenever I trained in the El Paso area, we had to make arrangements to fly in our sparring partners because there was nobody in New Mexico or West Texas that could box more than one round with me. Everyone in the area had already been destroyed by my left hook and nobody could keep up with my relentless middleweight pace. I had the speed of a middleweight and punched as hard as any heavy-handed heavyweight. We needed real ringers to come in that had good solid experience and could hang with me a few rounds. Most needed to have granite chins, because it was only a matter of a few seconds or minutes before my hook would start finding its bullseye. Even then, we always had to have replacements on call, because these guys were slick on getting the hell out of town after the first two sparring sessions. Sometimes they wouldn't even wait for their check to come in. Napoleon would tell me to ease up a bit so that we could keep them around and that good work was hard to find. Sometimes depending what mood I was in, I couldn't resist the temptation and I'd knock one of the sparring partners out dead cold, and then I'd have to rely on mitt work for the remainder of training camp before the fight.

Napoleon was a great mitt man. He was smooth and fast at catching sharp, crisp and deadly combinations. He usually had to wear two sets of elbow braces and wrist braces when he held for me, because I would literally knock his elbows and shoulders out of their sockets. Most times his wrists would swell and he would have to lay off for days at a time. People would come from all over town to watch our rehearsed routine on the mitts. To this day, I haven't found anyone to hold them as calculatedly as he did. It was a truly amazing spectacle to watch us work together—two artists making music with a set of gloves and pads.

When Connelly flew in for the fight the night before the weigh-in, Salami made sure to use his tricks of the trade and got him the longest and most painful flight to El Paso. I believe there were at least three layovers. I knew it had to be horrendous on his body and hopefully it made him lethargic. For a fighter who is already dealing with severe nerves before a fight, this is hell to endure. Your body demands rest and when it's deprived from that before a fight, your performance will suffer greatly.

The day of the weigh-in there was a sense of electricity throughout the air of El Paso. I was fighting on a big card at the Haskins Center. The Haskins Center was the legendary basketball arena of the 1966 NCAA basketball champions, who were led by the world-famous coach Don Haskins. As I showed up to the weigh-in, I knew that this is where I would have to begin fucking with Connelly's sleep-deprived mind. The way that worked best in my experience was to remain completely quiet and look through my opponent's eyes like a set of laser beams. I wasted no time and did just that. We both stepped on the scale in the 240s range. Both of us were ready, tense and nervous. They had us size each other up for the cameras and give a quick stare-down for television and photos. I had learned to never move my eyes first. I always stayed locked in until the officials came and separated us. When I stared into his pupils, I could see his eyes dilate. I could see the shades of brown and hazel around his pupils. I stared at the veins in his corneas and I saw the bags under his eyes from the loss of sleep from the trip. Then, like I had anticipated, it happened. His eyes drifted for that half second and he looked away first. I knew I now had him where I wanted him. I even noticed his knees were shaking uncontrollably. I had now officially got the adrenaline and the pre-murder goosebumps. I was ready to kill this motherfucker.

The weigh-ins in Texas are always these long, drawn-out affairs. The physicals and paperwork that the Texas Fight Commission makes you go through are extremely exhausting. I must have been there for another two hours waiting in line with the other fighters to turn in my paperwork. The commissioners treat you worse than a homeless beggar asking for shelter. They always had no sympathy or regard for the fighters. We were always treated like second-rate people for whatever reason, and to this very day I still can't figure it out.

When it all was finally said and done, I did a few television interviews and met with the newspaper reporters. I always went to my favorite reporter, Bill Knight, first, to show him respect. He was a stand-up guy who always wrote fair articles without an agenda. Many of the other writers that I talked to were negative and extremely critical. I thought, fuck them, give it to the guy that deserves it and has no agenda. By the end of the media circus, I would be dead tired. The nerves, combined with the hours of waiting and interviewing, was purgatorial. The night before a fight I could never sleep, so I would usually pop a couple Tylenol PMs and that would eventually help me drift off. I would always wake up a bit groggy, but the adrenaline would kick in the day of the fight and handle it.

The day of the fight was always the worst. I would eat a light breakfast and count down the hours before I would have to go report to the arena. We always had to show up around 4 P.M. I would usually have to wait for all the preliminary fights to get done before we could even start warming up. By that time in my career, my fight was the co-main event and I would usually start warming up about two fights before, to get a good sweat before walking out into the arena. When it was my time to go out onto the big stage, I wasted no time at all. I walked out and made quick work of good ole Johnny Boy. I knocked him out with a vicious body shot to the liver that had him waving in surrender as his face snarled and winced up in utter pain. I called that famous signature shot "La Fea," or "The Ugly Bitch." I loved hitting people with The Ugly Bitch. It became the Rodriguez signature punch. The fight ended early in the first round and we were all excited and ready to get the party started.

As I walked back into the dressing room, signing autographs along the way, I noticed a real aggravation on little Napoleon's face. There had been a lot of tension between us during training camp, and in the dressing room he told me, "I'm sick of you acting like you're God's gift to the world and women."

I looked at him and asked, "Why are you so pissed off? We just won. Come out tonight and let's blow off some steam. I'll buy the first few rounds!"

I couldn't understand why he was so aggravated. We had literally just won our first title. I didn't want it to tamper with my evening and win so I decided not to let it bother me. I assumed it was just some personal affair, so I overlooked it and got dressed, because I wasn't going to let him or anything else fuck up the good time that I had just earned. I had spent three months in training camp in preparation for this fight, and to me it was like getting released from prison.

After a little commotion and some disagreements, we all calmed down and walked over to the bar that was hosting my championship after party. I was dressed in a nice black button-up shirt with matching slacks while wearing my bright and shiny new Texas Heavyweight Championship belt. It was my friend Kevin's idea. I hated to show off, but my friends absolutely loved every second of it. I could tell showing off the belt aggravated Napoleon as well, so part of me loved wearing it to spite him. As the bar got crowded and drinks started to flow, Napoleon started to act disrespectful and violent.

He kept coming up to me saying, "Damn, bro, all these people are talking a ton of shit about you!"

I said, "Just ignore them, man. It's no big deal, let's get some ass tonight and have a good time!"

I put my arm around him and gave him a hug, but he knocked my arm off and walked away. I was beginning to get sick of his attitude and I didn't really give a shit if his panties were up in a wad, so I kept the party going with my friends Kevin, Sammy, Arty, Danny and Grady. It was a whole clan of us. We were a tight group of friends and nothing broke our bond. We would crack jokes and insult each other constantly, but if you were an outsider trying any of that with us, you would pay dearly for it. It was only an El Paso border boys thing, a kind of brotherhood. It was and still is a brotherhood that could never be broken despite our disagreements. We knew everyone at the bar and we were getting free bottle service the whole night long. Drinks were continuously flowing and the sounds of constant cheers and laughter masked the soon-to-be-growing tension in the air.

As the night went on, we started hearing random complaints from close friends and strangers about Napoleon's devious and aggressive behavior. Different men throughout the night were coming up to us, saying that they were going to knock him out if he didn't stop hitting on and bothering their girls. He was basically acting like a reckless hormonal teenager while losing full control of his drinking. My friends and I finally decided that enough was enough, so we rushed over to pull him away from one particular girl that was complaining about his behavior to her boyfriend. She had a distasteful look of disgust on her face as we pried him away from her personal space. He stuck his tongue out at her and moved it around his lips in a sexual manner while calling her a stuck-up bitch. She glanced away and stuck her index finger in her mouth and pretended to vomit and gag. Right when we started to grab him, he leaned back with a cocked fist and viciously punched her in the jaw. I stood there like a paralyzed deer caught by a vehicle's oncoming headlights while my body became numb in complete disbelief. She flew to the floor helpless, and then a commotion broke out all over the bar.

I couldn't believe my eyes. I had just witnessed my own once-respected trainer punch a woman in public. We all took initiative and helped her to her feet, but Napoleon wasted no time in the distraction and pushed people out of the way as he sprinted like a running back out of the bar. As my eyes circled around the bar I noticed the bouncers were all rushing and scrambling behind him like a gang of angry, bloodthirsty

wolves about to devour a lost and wounded sheep. Napoleon ran out of the bar and right out onto oncoming traffic as I saw the silhouette of a bouncer catch up to him and push him from behind. He landed headfirst in the street with cars screeching their brakes around him. The bouncer that made the game-winning tackle was my good buddy, Sammy "The Bull" Streep. He was bouncing that night while enjoying the celebration of victory with us.

I yelled, "Sammy! Let him go! That's my fucking trainer!"

Sammy looked at me in horror. "He just fucking hit a girl, Dave!"

"I know, Sammy, but I can't afford the bad press. You gotta understand that, please!"

As I begged and pleaded with the rest of the bouncers, Napoleon took advantage of the distraction once again and made a quick fast break toward the dark alleys and streets. All the bouncers ran after him once more, but ended up losing track of him in the late night darkness. I couldn't believe that I had a woman-beating coward for a trainer. All of a sudden, my opinion of him completely hit the floor. All the honor and respect that he had earned and developed with me over the years had just instantly vaporized into the thin night air.

I thought about my three sisters and mother. What would they want me to do about this? How would a real man handle this unbelievable and horrific altercation? All I knew was that this was a bad situation and that I was drunk. I didn't want the attention of bad press and I could hear the sirens coming at warp speed, so I decided I needed to get home fast. The last thing I wanted was to be questioned by the cops while intoxicated and be on the morning news. The bouncers were close friends of mine and promised to deflect the situation and cover for all of us.

I never felt the same about Napoleon for the duration of my career. I needed to get away from this piece of dog shit and at any cost. I answered no calls on the situation and we all covered for him by denying we even knew him. We denied he had any affiliation with my career and that he wasn't my trainer, and we all stuck to the story that we had orchestrated. The young girl never pressed charges, thanks to persuasion from her boyfriend and my close friends. I believe she was too embarrassed to follow through and also wanted no negative media attention. Her boyfriend had ended up being a good friend with a few of my close buddies, so the couple decided to let it fade away until the dust settles. They showed mercy and promised they were only showing sympathy for me, not for Napoleon. I understood this and made them a promise to get away from this deranged and ill-tempered lunatic. I planned my escape and from that day forward, you could cut the tension between us with a knife. This incident was the beginning of the downfall of our mutually-desired goal. Training in the gym with him after that night was filled with tension and disgust. I could not let myself listen or take instruction from a man for whom I no longer had any respect, but we did have a contract. I was now stuck between a rock and hard place with nowhere to go.

This was my first taste of salt in the boxing world. When you have disgust for a person you must work with daily for a desired goal, things begin to get messy. As I slowly learned about the characters that were involved with my career, I also started learning about the corrupt politics of the sport. My first title win was just a small taste of drama and of what was to come in the corrupt and dirty political world of boxing. I now started to realize that my honeymoon with the sport was over. I was in an abusive marriage with it.

CHAPTER 21

UNDERSTANDING THE ABCS OF BOXING, AND MY FIRST BIG CHAMPIONSHIP

I t took me years to learn the ropes of the politics of boxing, but boy, did I learn them well. In boxing there are thousands of organizations and sanctioning bodies claiming they have World Championship belts. Don't let that fool you. There are only three belts the public should be concerned with, and that's the three W's of boxing—WBC, WBA, and WBO. Nothing else. There are a few that are almost up to par, but not quite. Then there are hundreds of bullshit imitation belts that you win to gain some kind of clout, and then you abandon them so you don't have to keep paying sanctioning fees. It's pure boloney and hogwash. If you can sell it to an uneducated crowd by proclaiming that the belt you won is the real deal, then you can make the money at the gate to keep paying for the membership fees. It's a giant racket, and I'm sad to say there are cities across the country going through this exact dishonesty right now.

I know the minds behind this bullshit very well, and it's a con job. My management was called multiple times to fight for many unknown "world title championship" belts over the course of my career, but we always declined because that would make me look amateur to the other, bigger belts that really mattered. The three W's really want no affiliation or to be giving any kind of attention or credit to any other belts. They want to keep the boys' club, the boys' club. So always remember the three big W's of boxing: WBC, WBA, WBO.

As I was coming up, the three big W's had junior belts that were way bigger than any other world championship belts out there, because they let a boxer gain status and ranking in the organizations that really mattered. If you didn't feel you could win one of these legit junior titles, you would simply bow out and basically go buy yourself a world title belt; these were usually vacant because nobody wanted to pay the money to fight for something that would be career suicide. It's usually something that desperate and no-name fighters do in order to gain status among their peers and the ignorant media. There are literally hundreds of organizations to pick from. It's a joke, but if you can get a crowd to believe it, you can sell it. I didn't want that kind of short cut, nor did any of the other real fighters that I knew. We went the legit way. Fight the toughest, most talented fighters of your time, and make your mark in the three W's.

My two most memorable wins for belts were the WBC Mexican Heavyweight Championship, which put me in the top thirteen, and the WBA-NABA belt, which put me in the top twelve of that particular organization. I was also ranked #4 and #2 in other world belts that weren't even worth speaking of. Those were belts that I would never even think of fighting for. It would have been suicide for my career and I would have been frowned upon among the more serious organizations. The first legit belt I was ready to fight for was the NABA belt.

It was the biggest title in the WBA before the Heavyweight Championship of the World. It was an honor to contend for that title. I was scheduled to fight a rough Argentinian fighter with a record of 23-3. He would be, up to that point, my toughest test. He was not very fast, but he had good timing and a head that was as hard as a cement block.

The fight was scheduled to be held in Torreón, Mexico, and I was all over the media in my hometown. I was becoming a sensation. The fight would be televised on Mexican pay-per-view, and I was doing interviews with Televisa and Telemundo constantly. Once again, behind the scenes, I was a nervous wreck. I had to fly into Torreón a couple of weeks early for the media attention and press conferences. The city was on fire when I got there. Every day I would train in front of the media, eat my lunch at my hotel in front of the media, and then be followed around by the media the rest of the evening. It was exciting, but incredibly annoying. My team and I were finally making moves, and we were fast-tracking to the Heavyweight Championship of the World. I saw posters all over the city of myself and of my opponent: *Rodriguez vs. Pucheta for the NABA Heavyweight Championship*.

Napoleon was much more at ease by this time and wasn't having any more mental breakdowns or episodes around me. My guess was that he was starting to feel satisfied in the direction my career was heading, and he was making more money than I had initially thought he was. I still felt extremely disgusted with him, but I learned to tolerate it for the benefit and betterment of my career. I learned to keep a lid on everything. I felt it was best for our ultimate goal.

Before this fight, I began to get really close to Salami Slammer. I was confiding in him my very personal issues about my bouts with depression and extreme anxiety. He would always console me and give me a calming, confidence-building talk before every fight, right when I was just about to walk out into the arena. He was really starting to grow on me as a person and as a caring friend. Things were looking up, but I still hadn't received the revised contract that he had promised me. I was hoping that after this fight, we could renegotiate the whole damn thing that I had signed at the naïve age of twenty-one. During this time, I was also dealing with a handful of financial advisors that were starting to ask me serious questions about why certain money wasn't coming through. I was an undefeated heavyweight fighting on television, yet the numbers were not adding up. I had no answers.

A couple of days before the fight in Torreón, I was eating lunch and the Salami Slammer sat close and put his hand upon my knee. He started talking and seemed extremely upset with some issues about the promotion of the fight. I was starting to have the sense I was going to get fucked on this whole deal. It was in the air and every time he sat next to me to explain anything with his hand on my knee, it was usually bad news.

I asked him what the problem was and he replied, "These motherfuckers are making me nervous. I'm trying to get things locked down for the money we are asking." Yup, that was code for, "I'm about to screw you."

They always knew the right time to drop the bombs like that. It's always during intense and distracting situations, so you're not paying attention to the man behind the curtain. Knowing I needed to keep my cool before the fight, I just scooted back in my chair and closed my eyes.

I said, "Well, at least I have good sponsors."

He looked at me with those weasel eyes. I stopped him before he could speak any more and signaled that I just wanted to eat my food in peace. He nodded in agreement and told me to just focus on the task at hand and that the rest would work itself out. Our conversation started to lift and go into many different directions, and the mood finally started to ease a bit, but I was still feeling cheated.

I knew he could see my anger and frustration, but he kept trying to put me at ease. I had been guaranteed a certain amount of money, and then the purse got considerably lower, and now I was being told I couldn't keep the loyal sponsors that paid good money for the real estate on my trunks. I could see he was trying to calm me down, and he changed the subject. He wanted me calm and not infuriated before a major title fight. I needed to be calm and collected.

I brought up the disappointment my family would have for me, and how I'm sick of fighting for little to no money. I'm going into a major title fight and I'm not guaranteed the full amount of my purse? I had training expenses and living expenses and it was becoming a struggle to make boxing worthwhile. I kept imagining myself putting my fist through his skull because everything was becoming so clear and obvious to me now. Behind his grin and friendly pats on the back was a greed-filled serpent wanting more of the pie than he deserved. I just knew there had to be some backroom deals going on behind closed doors. I could feel my blood start to boil and my blood pressure rise, so I took a deep breath and centered myself.

I decided to excuse myself from the table and go back to my room to lie down to rest. I'd finally had enough of this roller coaster of a freak show reality. One of my trainers was a known woman-beater, and now I'm seeing this is basically slavery. I'm getting the feeling I'm fighting to fatten the pockets of everyone except me.

As I took the elevator, I started thinking about Napoleon

and his issues, and now the thoughts of getting short-changed in Mexico for a title fight started to flood my mind and emotions. This was not the mental state I wanted to be in before a giant title fight. I just wanted to fight and get home to my see my family and friends. When I exited the elevator, I noticed my opponent standing next to my hotel room door. I looked at him in confusion. He just winked at me and opened the door next to mine. We were staying at the Marriot and the hotel was huge. There was no way he just coincidentally had a room next to mine. My stomach began to get queasy as I opened the door to my room. I knew things like this happened in the boxing world and I knew it had to be mind games. This is when I understood his tactic. He must have requested the room next to mine in order to begin the mind games. He wanted to be in my space and in my head, twenty-four-seven. He wanted me mentally exhausted before I entered the ring. This was a very clever war tactic, but it wasn't going to work on me. I prepared too long and too hard for this moment and I was ready for anything he could bring.

When I laid down on my bed, I started to think about my preparation and the long road it took to get to this very moment. I began thinking of my fans, friends, and family. Everyone who ever supported me. Thoughts of my childhood experiences overcame my mind. All the days of eating my lunch in a stall out of fear. All the times I ran away from kids chasing me to beat me up at the bus stop. All these childhood moments crept into my mind and then the sudden realization hit me like a wrecking ball. I made it through all of those terrifying and humiliating experiences to be here at this very moment, fighting for a NABA-WBA heavyweight championship. This could be my last and final stop until I'm actually fighting for the one-man Super Bowl. The Heavyweight Championship of the World. This was the last belt to win until the big dance. There was no going back. Everything in my life had led me to this very moment. I knew after this fight I would have to come to the heartbreaking decision to leave my team. I wasn't being treated fairly and the fact that I was being cheated out of my money was finally enough. I made up my mind that shortly after this fight, I would begin to break the ties with my slave owners. The promoter wasn't exactly my favorite either. He pretended to smile and shower me with hugs, but I knew he had ulterior motives. I wasn't being treated like the superstar he kept talking me up to be.

I wasn't being treated like the promoters' favorite, and I was certainly not getting paid like it. The whole time I laid in my bed, I could hear my opponent right through the walls, talking on the phone, using the toilet, and using the sink. I tried calling the front desk to move rooms for my peace of mind, but the hotel was booked to capacity due to the fight. I felt alone and was now stuck in this uncomfortable and nightmarish environment and situation. The most awkward part of this whole dilemma was when we both walked out of our rooms at the exact same time to use the elevator. This became a routine, because we would eat at the same times and do press at the same times. Every time we walked out to use the elevators, there was a silence once the elevator doors closed that was so uncomfortable, you could hear a mouse fart.

As the time came for the fight, I felt ready to knock his ass out, not only for making my living situation hell, but because his snores were like a freight train on a dirt road. When it was time for the fight, I was surprised we took separate cars to the arena. I got so used to this guy's presence that I almost thought about splitting the cab fare to the arena with him. When fight time came, I honestly began to feel like I was going to fight my newly-estranged roommate.

We walked out of our rooms one last time and gave each other the final last glare of predators ready to attack their prey. We were both fed up with our accommodations, and we were ready to kill each other. When I checked in to the arena, I had the mindset of a killer. I wanted to destroy and annihilate my opponent, but I was also disgusted with my entire team for allowing these unusual circumstances. I wanted to turn into an atomic bomb and blow up the whole arena with everyone in it. I was angry, but I knew I couldn't enter the ring that way. I needed to focus and stick to my game plan of being the calculated killer. I warmed up well and broke a beautiful sweat throughout my body. My muscles were warm and glistening with the hard work of sweat. I was hitting the hand pads hard and extremely fast. I felt great, better than I ever had, and I was about to give the fans what they came to see. They were about to see two well-conditioned Spartans fight to the death. The moment of anticipation had finally arrived. My next-door neighbor and I were up next. It was showtime.

As I walked out into the tunnel to get ready for my entrance, the appearance of television cameras overtook my personal space. Three cameras blocked my entrance and the television crew came out and pointed at the red tape by my feet. They wanted me to stand there until my song came on so they could time my entrance. Then one of the commissioners stopped and yelled at me to let my opponent walk by first. I now knew I was the promoters' favorite because I was the last to enter the ring. As Pucheta walked by, he locked eyes with me and we stared at each other with intense hatred. This guy was ready and meant business. He entered the ring with his corner men while waving the Argentinian flag to loud blaring music. It reminded me of the beginning of a soccer game at the World Cup. The crowd went ballistic. He was very proud and he had come to fight hard for his country. Mexican and South American fighters are like this. It's very serious business to them. They'd rather die than lose the respect of their countrymen.

I watched for a moment with a weirdly newfound respect, and then my music started to play. It was time. We all started the single-file walk to the most honest place on earth. My corner yelled and clapped as we made our way through the screaming crowd and into the ring. I made it up the steps and climbed through the ropes, revealing myself under the bright lights. It must have been 110 degrees under those damn lights. I could hear the crowd go up in a roar when my music stopped and they knew the action was about to start. The crowd was so deafening that I couldn't even hear the announcer. I was hopping up and down to keep warm as he screamed to introduce us. I just knew my cue would be to lift my arm in pride when the announcer looked over and pointed in my direction. Most of the Hispanic crowd was cheering for Pucheta. After his long and drawn-out introduction, he lifted his arm in pride and made a polite bow to the crowd while his corner draped the Argentinian flag over his rounded, cinderblock-looking shoulders. I stared at him during the instruction and noticed his intimidating solid stalky frame, yet I couldn't take my eyes away from his extremely large bouncing man-breasts. He was solid as rock all over his body, except for the pair of huge bouncing man boobs. They kept bouncing up and down like water balloons as he jumped around and made faces in the ring.

After the Argentinean anthem and the Mexican anthem had played, it was finally time to get it on. We stood across the ring from each other, staring each other over in nervous excitement and anticipation. Both of us knew we wanted to make a strong and powerful statement early. I felt I could knock him out quickly. There was no way he was going to take one of my precision body shots, especially after the warm up I had had in the dressing room. Before the bell was about to ring, I made the sign of the cross and pointed to the sky for my beautiful sister, who had lost her battle to alcoholism a year prior. I usually always heard her screaming and yelling in the rafters of the crowd, but this time I only felt her in my heart. I said to myself, "I know you're here, Patrice. Please take care of me and guide me to victory in this battle."

As soon as I finished saying those words, the bell rang. We both charged out like bulls. I threw the first combination and I landed a good one on his hard head. I reeled back for a moment. It felt like I had just broken my hand on his Neanderthal skull. He kept snorting and coming forward like a raging bull, while throwing looping hard shots to my head and ribs. Seconds later, I felt a sharp sting and heard a crack. I knew he must have broken my ribs. I could feel his monster knuckles through his gloves. Every time he punched me it hurt, and every time I landed clean shots on him, it hurt just as badly.

DING DING! The bell rang to end the first round. I went back to my corner knowing this was going to be a very long night. My hand was swelling up and so were my ribs. Every time I tried to suck in air, I felt a knife go through my right side. As I looked across into his eyes at the corner, I could see that he was just fine. I was the one hurting.

I got up to start round two, and we met again in the middle of the ring. I decided it was time to let my punches go and end this motherfucker before he started getting too much confidence. I hit him with six clean punches. BAM BAM BOOM BING BAM BOOM!! I stepped back to examine my work and see if he showed any kind of weakness. He didn't. He just kept snorting like a bull and pressing forward.

I wanted to panic, but I knew I had to remain calm. I

had twelve rounds to work, so I needed to start breaking him down a bit. I started going to the body. BOOM BAM BOOM. Nothing. He would just take a step back and lift his hands up to taunt me to the crowd and then he would press forward again. After a few more rounds of this went by, I noticed that every time I hit him to the body, he took a step back and acted like a clown to the crowd. This was meant to get inside my mind, but I was smarter than that. I knew through experience that when fighters start relying on these types of tactics, it usually means they're hurt and hiding it. As the fight went on, he continued with these antics. I was breathing hard and heavy and I could feel my hands, face, and right side swelling. Yet he continued to step back and act like a clown every time I landed a tremendous shot to his gut. I decided to focus solely on his belly because his head was a block of concrete and my hands couldn't take any more punishment. I landed "La Fea" on his left side and I saw him wince and take a step back to wave at the crowd.

Holy shit. Could it be?

I had found his sweet spot, and decided that the next time I cracked him to the body, I would press forward and put more pressure on him. He came forward and dipped down a bit, accidentally exposing his body. My fist slammed into his left side and I knew it fucking hurt him. Once he stepped back, I jumped on him with hands rapid-fire and blazing. He covered up and waited for me to punch myself out. He played possum a bit and waited for me to finish my assault. I realized then that he was tough and wasn't going to let up that easy. He felt he had figured me out, so he started covering up every time I barged in after a staggering body attack. The fight turned into a high-speed strategic chess match. We had to outwit each other to create the opening we both wanted.

We were going into the seventh round and my punches had lost major steam. I was running out of tricks to hit him with, but as we came out, he looked tired and was gasping for air, holding his hands lower by his sides. I knew those body shots had to be taking their toll. My body shots knocked out most men, but this guy was cut from a different cloth. His body looked fat, but he took a body shot better than most guys with sculpted, eight-pack abdominals. I decided to try something different. I feinted my routine body shot and pivoted off to the side, while throwing a sharp and crisp left hook to his chin. BING! I hit him right on the sweet spot and he went down for the first time in the fight. I ran to the neutral corner so the referee could start the ten count.

The referee got mid-count before Pucheta got up and signaled for me to come back and bring him some more. He looked pissed and ready to trade punches with me. This was now do or die. Before I tiredly staggered from the neutral corner to launch my attack, I took a deep breath and spoke to my sister. "Okay, Patrice, I really need you right now."

I stepped forward and went full force, launching my relentless attack. I couldn't let him recover. I had to get him out of there. I threw about fifteen punches as he fired back himself a little, but mainly he decided to take cover. Then, WAM! He dropped down to his knees while looking up at me in exhaustion. The referee then stepped in and waved off the fight. I closed my eyes in calm and said a quick thank you to my sister and to Jesus Christ for His deliverance. I was now only one step away from the WBA Heavyweight Championship of the World.

The crowd rose in a standing ovation! I ran to the other side of the ring with my hands up in the air and I could feel my whole corner surrounding me. The crowd was in a complete frenzy. After many objects of gratitude got thrown into the ring, I realized I had just done it. A warm, calm feeling came over me as my hands were lifted in victory. Moments later, the announcer signaled the WBA representatives into the ring. They told me to lift my hands up even higher as they put the beautiful golden NABA strap around my waist. I gazed up into the sky the entire time, saying thank you to God and to my beautiful sister. "Thank you so much Patrice. I love you." Then I blew kisses up to the sky and made my way out of the ring.

That night, I didn't go out and party. I simply laid in bed and stared at my beautiful new belt. This was my girlfriend for the night. I didn't care about the groupies waiting outside my dressing room. I wanted to be alone with my championship accomplishment. It was my moment. It was my small slice of heaven and I wanted to savor every last second of it. Everything had been worth it. I may have been cheated out of my full purse, but this moment was priceless. It was my fourth belt and it was the biggest. I knew that I would be a ranked world contender and it felt utterly amazing to be recognized among the elite fighters of the world. Dreams do come true.

CHAPTER 22

THE BREAKUP AND MY COMEBACK

David Rodriguez knocking out Robert Davis with his signature left hook

After the plane ride back home, I was greeted by fans at the airport in El Paso. It was a nice coming home party... except for one thing. I never got my paycheck. I also wasn't allowed to wear my sponsors on my robe or trunks due to a conflict of interest with the promotional sponsors they already had for the fight. Basically, I made no money for knocking out Pucheta to win the NABA Heavyweight Championship.

I went home and it started festering slowly inside me. I was beginning to get fed up with headlining the tough fights for Salami's shows in Texas and other places for minimum pay. I made more money in high school throwing parties at Juárez clubs than doing this bullshit. All of the stress, combined with the exploitative nature of my contract, was starting to burden me and freak me out. The contract with Salami that I signed when I was twenty-one was a joke. Salami took 33% for management, while my trainer Napoleon took his 10% and another 5% off of Salami Slammer's side. There was also another 10% to be taken off the top for my training expenses, which were very vaguely defined in the contract. In short, I was clearly getting fucked.

One time, Salami called me up to fight a big contender for $75,000 on HBO. After doing the math, I would see 53% of that money gone right away. Then add in the taxes after the splits, and I would make nothing. I started pleading with him to renegotiate my contract, but at that point he had too much money invested in me and he wanted his money back. All the big fights were starting to get thrown my direction, but my contract was terrible. I wasn't about to go fight tough fights like a field slave to make money for other people. Something had to be done, but every time I called Salami, he would get nervous, then start to stutter and yell in frustration at me over the phone. He wouldn't even have the balls talk to my father or mother, much less my lawyer. Then he started ignoring my calls. I knew I had to do something, but what?

As much as I hated doing so, I called our family lawyer to get involved and to ask the necessary questions. Nothing threatening, just legitimate questions. He called and left messages multiple times. There was no return phone call. After months of having no response back from him and no fights scheduled, I had no option but to send him a cease and desist letter from my attorney. He never responded with any kind of rebuttal. He just disappeared. Although I thought it was completely odd, it was a relief, not having the monkey on my back any longer.

After that, I decided to call Napoleon to see if he would still be interested in training me. He stayed quiet on the phone for a while and said, "Well, I want 25% of your contract then." I said, "What the hell? That's more than any trainer should get! Trainers only get 10%!" I tried bargaining with him and told him I would give him 15% because I knew his value, but I couldn't go any higher than that. He got extremely argumentative and hardheaded and kept blurting out, "No!"

I hung up the phone and couldn't believe that a thirteen-year-long, loyal relationship with this team had finally come to a disastrous end. I felt extremely liberated, but I was still in shock and depressed deep down inside. What I thought was real for so many years was nothing but a con. Never in my life had I been the sucker or on the losing end of a good money deal, but this time I was the fool. The more I thought about it, the more I suspected that Napoleon had a bigger cut with Salami than I had originally thought. Nothing else made sense.

After a disastrous six months snuck by, I decided I needed to resume training again, but I had no one to train or manage me. I found myself with no direction again. That familiar old depression started to creep back in and hit me like a wrecking ball. It hit me harder than any opponent ever could. After thirteen years of stimulation and adrenaline, I was once again at rock bottom. I was ranked a top world contender, yet I had nobody to trust or turn to. I was emotionally shattered and betrayed. Nobody was even calling me, which seemed very odd. Then I found out exactly why.

Napoleon and Salami had teamed up together for a smear campaign of my name to my hometown and boxing world, saying I was scared to fight certain fighters and that I was really just a fraud. A fraud? A guy that's 33-0, with thirty-one knockouts, is a fraud? Who would believe these guys? Apparently they were very convincing. I was feeling the bullying I once gone through as a child return, but this time I didn't know how to fight back. My name was being tarnished. I had news anchormen calling me from certain networks to tell me about the hate emails they were receiving from my former team. I was horrified and absolutely embarrassed. I could not believe the depths those two would sink to.

After the weeks, then months, of hearing horrendous lies and rumors about me, I had built up a severe bitterness and anger for my former team, and for boxing in general. I had to do something quickly. My career and reputation were at risk. One day I got a ring on the telephone. It was a fast-talking and good-spirited, charismatic guy that I'll call "Z." Z was very positive over the phone, and had had some local shows in El Paso a few times. He had some connections with the WBC and WBA, so he offered his help. It was 2010 and I had only fought once, at the very beginning of the year, knocking out the Brazilian gold medalist. That was the last fight I had with my old team and I needed to get busy or I was going to keep free-falling in the sanctioning rankings. Z told me he knew a trainer and that we could get started immediately. He was talking about the legendary cut man Rafael Garcia.

Rafael was the cut man for Floyd Mayweather and had worked with many other world champions. He trained out in Vegas, so we needed to figure things out and fast. Wasting no time, I took the long drive out to see Z and to meet with Rafael Garcia at a Starbucks on the outskirts of Vegas. Rafael Garcia was the most stylish, coolest older gentleman I have ever met. We got along immediately. He was so kind, like a long-lost grandfather. He always wore his trademark hat, with his collection of a thousand gold and silver buttons all over it.

He was in his early eighties at the time, and was still a rare diamond in the boxing world. We wanted to set up a fight as early as February, so we had to hurry up and begin training. He did not want me rusting and becoming stagnant. It would be too expensive this first time around to train in Vegas, so we decided to have my first training camp held in El Paso.

Joe Sullivan came to my aid once again. He knew a really well-known mitt man in the area, so he took me to see him. His name was Herman "The Hitman" Delgado and he was one funny SOB. Herman was a blunt, don't-take-no-shit type of guy, and a pretty good heavyweight back in the '90s. I knew of Herman from my early days and was actually quite fond of the guy already. He would literally say whatever that was on his mind, and you could go fuck yourself if you had anything to say about it. In a weird way I respected that type of attitude and I guess it goes as far back as when I had my pet rooster. I had admired a no-shit-taking attitude since I was a child.

The new energy we all had together was fresh, invigorating, and magical. I realized I didn't need Salami or little Napoleon after all. Now the only thing on my mind was that I just needed to prove it. I needed to prove it to myself, and to the people around me who still believed. Simply feeling this way wasn't enough. I needed to fight and I needed to win in a big way. I needed to get back in the ring and knock off the rust.

After careful planning, Z contacted a matchmaker by the name of Guy. Guy had a good eye for making fights and knew exactly what kind of fighter we needed. We needed a big, strong guy who was tough, but not too dangerous to risk everything we worked for in front of my hometown. I was coming off months of inactivity and rust. We needed to get El Paso excited about the homegrown, future heavyweight champion they possessed. Guy knew just the right opponent. His name was Matt Hicks, an ex–Dallas Cowboys football player with a respectable, solid record. He was big and strong, and was passing his prime as a fighter at the age of thirty-six. He had a 13-5 record and wanted to make a statement as well, by fighting and trying to embarrass me in front of my hometown.

Now that we had the opponent picked, it was time to train and get busy. This was the first fight without my old handlers, so I had a lot to prove to myself and to them. It was a completely new type of clean and good energy. Boxing was fun again and training was an absolute blast. Herman brought a lighthearted feeling to the training camp. Every day the training was serious, but his constant vulgar jokes and wisecracks made for an entertaining experience. Herman and I trained hard every day and we incorporated new methods of working out. We flipped huge tractor tires, and every other day we worked on hitting the tires with a sledgehammer. My shoulders would burn with fatigue and I could feel them getting stronger and stronger. My father became my new manager and financed the necessary sparring we needed to come to El Paso. My dad was finally back in the picture and playing a major role in my boxing life, and I knew he loved every second being around his son.

February came at warp speed, and it was finally time for the big homecoming fight in El Paso. The hype was in the air. I would be fighting in front of my hometown fans and supporters. It was amazing. The arena was packed. About 3,700 people were there just to see me get back in the ring and knock someone out. The curiosity had built up after my year away from boxing. People came to see one thing, a big knockout.

The fight went exactly as we had anticipated. The bell rang and I got busy. I wanted it to be a good show for El Paso. We traded punches a little bit, but he had nothing. I went right through him like a hot knife through butter. It was over as fast as it had started. I punched his forearm and broke it. He tried to cover my relentless body attack and his arm got in the way. He took a knee and started yelling and pointing to his forearm. He quit right there in front of a bloodthirsty and screaming crowd. I was ecstatic, not only because I won, but because I did it without the old Tweedledee and Tweedledum dipshits. I hugged Herman and Rafael Garcia with tears rolling down my cheeks, and then I spoke to the news stations promising to be El Paso's first World Heavyweight Champion!

That night, I had a bunch of very good friends visiting in town from Dallas. They all flew in to see my fight. They weren't the usual entourage I ran with, but I had so many people around me that a few more couldn't hurt. They were all a group of good-looking, alpha male Dallas socialites with all the connections to the big clubs and parties. We were a group of unstoppable, heartbreaker sluts of men. We were like modern-day Vikings and our energy together was ridiculous. There must have been eight of them there that night and we were all ready to get the post-fight celebration week started. We had a small warm-up party in El Paso the first night, then they had planned a huge victory celebration in Dallas the following night at some new club that had just opened up. I was back in the boxing scene and floating on cloud nine. I was an undefeated 34-0 heavyweight with thirty-two big knockouts. Nobody and nothing could touch the invincibility I felt. I was back to feeling superhuman. I just wanted to get to Dallas, get my celebration on, and then return to training camp to do it all over again. But the night in Dallas would prove to be very different from what I expected.

CHAPTER 23

THE GRIM REAPER KNOCKS
FOR THE FIRST TIME

By the time I boarded the plane to Dallas, I was a drunken mess. I even ordered more drinks on the plane to make sure my stupor would still be intact by the time I arrived in Dallas. I was juggling two extremes, heavy training and heavy drinking. I just didn't know how to turn off the adrenaline. I constantly needed the stimulation. I was like a shark that had to keep moving or else it would die. If I slowed down, my demons would attack me and I would have to face them down. I learned that staying in perpetual motion was best. I had to keep the adrenaline flowing and flowing fast. I didn't want to stop and have to face down my severe depression. Whenever a fight was over, I knew depression was lurking just around the corner, so partying and women had to be the answer until training camp would start again. I needed boxing, alcohol, sex and drugs to keep me stimulated. I was leading a very exhausting life, burning the candle at both ends and burning it fast.

When I arrived in Dallas, it was go time. My friends picked me up with beers already in hand. As we drove to my buddy's house to change, my hands were still swollen from the fight, so I decided to take a few painkillers. As I got changed to hit the celebration party, I was still drinking. I actually had a bottle of vodka in the shower with me. After we all changed, we drank some more, and jumped up and down like animals. Then we piled into Jake's Tahoe and headed to the club.

We rolled up and there was a line wrapped around the entire building. The place was loud and the atmosphere was intense. We made our way in and Ricky came running up to me and started pouring tequila down my throat. We all laughed and I asked where the vodka was at. I poured myself a deep glass of it. We had our own booth and I already had a few girls sitting with me as my own personal party favors. At one point, I started talking to a sweet girl named Michelle. She looked like she was observing me through the lens of an anthropologist. I'm surprised I didn't scare her off—I was acting like a raging animal. I was chugging down the vodka and taking shot after shot of tequila. I was full of adulation and satisfaction from my comeback knockout. I was riding cloud nine and the celebration was well overdue.

The partying went full speed and my heart started pounding. I felt clammy and warm and I started sweating profusely. I ignored it because I didn't have time for that. I wanted to let loose and meet some more ladies. I'd been training my ass off for three months straight, and now it was time to unwind and throw my cares to the world. When I trained, I wouldn't have one sip of alcohol. I was strict in training camp, so letting loose and having a few drinks was my reward after a strenuous training camp and fight. It was a kind of soul-cleansing therapy to me. I had been clean and healthy for months, so I really didn't think anything of it. Partying like a raging lunatic after a fight was my way of letting go and getting it out of my system until the next training camp and fight. I kept the drinks flowing like a college kid on his first outing with his fraternity brothers. I started to drip with sweat while my heart pounded faster, and then even faster, and I didn't know the reason why.

I felt a tap on my left shoulder. It was a bodybuilding acquaintance that I had partied with many times in Dallas. We gave each other a hug, and I said to him, "I'm not feeling my best, My adrenaline is still pounding from the fight."

He said, "I got just the thing for you, my bro." I told him not to give me any cocaine. He looked at me, smirked, and said, "Nah bro, this is GHB. It will help relax you a bit."

He pulled a flask out of his jacket pocket and handed it to me. Before he could say anything, I grabbed it out of his hand and chugged the whole damn flask. Last thing I remember of him was his face painted in terror. I had no idea you're only supposed to take a small cap full of it, because it's an extremely potent drug. When I tried to hand the flask back, he was gone, nowhere to be found.

I was nervous as I made my way back to the VIP booth. The moment I sat down, I began getting blurry vision and my heart went from a racing pace to slow, pounding beats. I started to look around and the club started to fade in and out. People would talk to me, but I couldn't hear anything besides the sound of a bass beating inside my chest. I started panicking and scanning the club for my friends. I told a buddy what was going on, but he just started laughing real loud and smacking me on the shoulder, telling me it was all right. Confused, I walked to another buddy, but he did the same exact thing. They were drunk themselves and they wanted no distractions from their good time. I couldn't find Roger, so I sat down in my booth and my head fell into my hands in hopelessness.

I was now spinning and my breathing was becoming

faint. People said, "Leave him alone, he's just drunk." Then I could hear the girl next to me asking me questions with a blurry look of panic and concern on her face. I started to help-lessly drool out of the corners of my mouth like a two-year-old. My surroundings began closing in and getting smaller,

smaller

smaller

and then

good bye.

The night went something like this, according to Michelle's account. She told me later that she was the one that saved my life and that my own friends didn't give a fuck about me. She was the one who frantically ran to get help from all my Dallas friends. None of them wanted to help. They thought I was just drunk and told her to let me sleep it off. She saw that I was turning blue and my pulse was weakening. She ran to the bouncers, but they didn't care either. She couldn't find anyone willing to help me. Everybody was too interested in continuing the party, and if I was on the brink of dying, then it was my problem. She rubbed ice all over my face as I laid unconscious, a river of drool pouring out of my mouth. She finally found Roger and said, "Look at your fucking friend on the ground! He's fucking *dying*, Roger!"

Roger didn't know what to do, so he grabbed my friend Darrell to help get me outside. They tried to pick me up, but had no success. I was 250 pounds of dead weight. After they attempted that a few more times, eight very large bouncers came running over to help with the task. They began moving me slowly out to the side door by the back alley, dropping me multiple times along the way. Once they got my lifeless body to the alley, they threw me outside, headfirst. I'm guessing they didn't want the liability. I laid there for minutes, motionless.

It was an unspecified amount of time later that Roger, Michelle, and Darrell sped around the back to the alley in Michelle's friend's family-sized van. They teamed up and dragged me inside the van and sped to the hospital at 110 miles per hour, weaving in and out of traffic. According to Michelle's and Roger's accounts, they thought I had already died because my pulse was nonexistent. Darrell was supposedly the one who held me up as I laid across the backseat and kept talking with me, telling me to stay with him and not to die. Obviously, I remember none of this.

They raced into the emergency room, screaming, "Our friend is dying!" The paramedics came running out, saw me, and immediately started pumping my chest and performing CPR. After some success, they rolled me onto a gurney and rushed me into the hospital. When I went into cardiac arrest, they inserted a breathing tube down into my lungs.

After what could have been an eternity, I opened my eyes in sheer panic and saw a swarm of doctors all around me with masks on. There were bright lights shining into my eyes and the sounds of hospital machinery all around me. I was completely disoriented. I felt a tube get ripped out from my lungs and throat and I gasped for air. In complete panic I yelled, "Where am I? What's going on? Who are you guys?" Then I had the uncomfortable feeling of a catheter being ripped out from my johnson. I yelled and began punching the air. The doctors all spread out of the way and started yelling for me to calm down while trying to explain the situation.

I was scared. Was I in a car accident? Did I get knocked out during my fight? I looked down at my legs to make sure I still had them. I wiggled my toes. OK, check. How about my face? I asked for a mirror. Was my face okay? Yes, check. I frantically looked around the hospital room in fear. A few doctors calmed me down. One sat next to me and began explaining to me exactly what I had in my system, and all the reasons why I should have died. I turned toward him in tears and I asked why he didn't just let me go. I told him that he was only postponing the inevitable. He looked at me in shock and walked out of the I.C.U. He called in a twenty-four-hour nurse to do a mandatory suicide watch over me. She was a very nice and religious black lady that stayed with me for three days in ICU and another four days after they moved me to another hospital room. She did nothing but read her Bible and pray over me from time to time for the remainder of the time I was there.

While lying in the hospital bed for days, I realized that I had bigger demons than I could ever face down by myself. I knew I had issues that needed to be dealt with, but being so stubborn, I also knew I had to get ready to get back in training camp in just a couple of weeks. This incident was not going to stop me or slow me down. I needed to check out of there immediately and get ready for training camp. I was scheduled to fight Owen Beck, the former #1 contender of the world, in just a few short months, and I needed to get prepared. Staying in the hospital and not working out would only set me back from getting in the proper shape I needed. I stayed a few more days in the hospital, and then checked myself out against all of the doctors' recommendations. This minor setback was not going to stop me from having a WBC title to win!

I began training camp less than a week after suffering cardiac arrest and almost death. This time, I chose Vegas to train, because I didn't want to hear from my parents how I should take it easy and rest. I wanted nothing and nobody to get in my way. I wanted to win and win big. I was on a fast track to the Heavyweight Champion of the World. There was no time for excuses. My new team set up training camp the first two months in Vegas, and I sparred with the likes of Bermane Stiverne, a top heavyweight contender who later became the WBC Heavyweight Champion. He was powerful and tough, but we were sparring four-minute rounds at my trainer's request. I believe that played with his endurance mentally. Rafael Garcia loved me sparring four- to five-minute rounds. He knew at some point I would either catch my adversary with a good shot, or they would just flat-out quit. I daily beat the living tar out of every sparring partner I had. It got to the point that the other coaches would throw fits and yell at their protégés in disgust.

As the month of the Owen Beck fight arrived, I was ready. It was for the WBC Mexican Heavyweight Championship— one of their most prestigious belts before the Heavyweight Championship of the World. All I knew was that this guy was as slick as owl shit and that he threw a lot of punches, never tiring. I knew in my gut what I had to do. I needed to catch his shots defensively and find a way to come back counter, working him into position for my fast left hook. I didn't want to get caught up at his pace and leave myself open. It was going to be much smarter to catch and roll and then to fire back when I saw openings. We grinded on this routine every day in sparring and on the mitts. The trainer would throw five to six shots at a time at me, and I would cover and roll and then smash his mitts with three to four fast and precise punches.

After a couple months in the Vegas heat, I flew into El Paso a couple weeks early before the fight for media appearances. Z did a great job putting the fight together in El Paso. Everything was in order and ready to go. The weigh-in came and went, and even though Owen tried to look intimidating, I saw right through him. He was just another victim that had just willingly signed his death warrant. I was on a mission to

Crashing left hook

get back my respect and he was just my next obstacle. I entered the ring a fit 249 and he entered somewhere in the upper 230s. We were fighting in the Haskins center with a packed house of 4,000 people. This particular fight was going to get me ranked in the WBC elite for sure. We both climbed into the ring.

The bell rang. DING DING. He came out swinging. He threw extremely fast, stinging jabs that I kept catching with my glove over my face like a baseball mitt, so he started throwing faster combinations. Somehow, I blocked all of it. Nothing landed clean on me. Everything we had worked on in Vegas seemed to be working instinctively. It was like Floyd Mayweather took over my body that night. I was defensive, clever, and sharp. I was just waiting for the exactly right moment to let my hook go. It's like I had a wound-up coil in my arm just waiting for release.

The bell rang for the third round. He was still throwing most of his punches with confidence, but nothing was landing

Owen Beck lies motionless

clean. I noticed he would throw a clean combination and then pull back with his head in the air, leaving himself wide open. After I watched him do this a few times, I saw my opening. Without hesitation I let that coil go and launched my explosive double hook, BAM BAM! Two swift short left hooks that hit him squarely on the chin. He collapsed, out cold, no reason to even start the ten count. The doctors rushed in to give him oxygen and medical attention.

After a few moments of celebration, the crowd went silent. You could hear a pin drop. This had now turned serious. He wasn't moving. He looked lifeless as blood poured out of his nose and ears. He wasn't showing any signs of movement. More paramedics climbed into the ring. I became concerned and dropped to my knee in prayer to God to please not let this man die from my hands. Right there, in fear, I promised God that I would quit boxing forever if I had killed that man in the ring. He remained lifeless, no movement except for the occasional

Raphael Jr., Daniel Ybanez, David Rodriguez, Raphael Sr., and Herman Delgado

foot twitch. I knew this had to be serious head trauma and that if he were to survive, he should never box again.

After more time passed by, he started showing life and the paramedics lifted him up to his feet. He was down for ten minutes total. It was the single scariest punch I've ever landed on somebody in my career. The crowd rose to their feet and started applauding. I cautiously walked over to him and hugged him. I said, "Don't box any more, Owen. That was way too serious of a head injury and you need to never get hit again." He was still very disoriented and left the ring to make his way to the hospital. After the fight was over, my dad and mother climbed into my corner to hug me. I said, "I did this for Patrice, Mom!" She laid her head on my shoulders and began hugging and kissing me.

As I started my walk down the steps, some wild-eyed, crazed spectator came running up to me with the intent to spoil my victory. He shoved a flyer in my face that said mean and hateful things about my career. It had the looks of another smear campaign with my former team's signature all over it. I glanced it over for a second and then began to laugh out loud. I had just knocked out the former #1 contender of the world. I pushed the man out of my way and tore the paper in half. I looked around the arena and I noticed that the people obviously didn't care, because the pamphlets were all scattered around the floor. The only person that would have taken time out of their weasel little life for a smear campaign against me would have been Napoleon. However, I was elated and relieved that the biggest fight of my life was completed. I had a post-fight press conference to attend, and I had bigger and better things to worry about than someone's ridiculous envy. I had just solidified myself as a legit world contender once again. I was now on my way and nothing was going to stop me.

CHAPTER 24

ONE MORE CHAMPIONSHIP
WHILE WE WAIT

2011 was a roller coaster of a year and I was beaming with excitement. I had overdosed and almost died, only to somehow come back against all the doctors' orders or any kind of needed therapy and win the WBC Mexican Heavyweight Championship. I was back in top contention and thought, why stop there? Let's go for another minor belt while I wait for the bigger offers to start pouring in.

I was contacted by a smaller organization that had me ranked in the top twenty of their belt. They wanted me to fight for their North American belt. I didn't see why not, so we scheduled a fight for December as a "tune-up" against a tough Midwestern fighter by the name of Byron Polly. I decided to take this fight to stay active and out of trouble. I didn't want any more time to pass as I sat around waiting for phone calls from the world champions.

Byron was a rugged guy, but was a little on the round side. He was tough and his face showed the scars of ring wars and beatings. He wasn't talented, but he knew how to hang in for a long fight if you didn't have the skill to get him out of there early. His body was horrific-looking and was built like a pear. His body would be my prime target. What his body lacked, we knew his heart made up for. He always came to fight and put on a good show. He was known as a real crowd pleaser where he was from. If his talent was compared to a baseball player's, he would be the guy that goes back and forth from triple-A to the majors, never really earning his rightful position. Still, he was tough and hungry for an upset. He was coming to prove he belonged and if I didn't get him out early, it could make for a long and disastrous night.

December rolled around and we flew him into El Paso to hype up the press conference. We wanted to get the hype started and get the city excited early. This would be my final stop before fighting a top-five contender or a heavyweight champion of the world. We knew this would possibly be my last big fight in El Paso before the next huge fight on the horizon.

Byron knew what was at stake and he actually came looking in shape, for him. His face at least looked trim, until he took off his shirt—and that's when you could hear the crowd gasp in disbelief. It looked as if he trained on a diet of hot-dogs and pizza. At the press conference everything looked to be going smooth. I was in good spirits and answering all necessary questions from the media. I spoke at the podium, very cordial and polite, and promised El Paso a win on my way to the championship of the world. Then Byron Polly got to the podium and he was very emotional. He started gasping and expressing his deeply-harbored feelings about the recent passing of his son. As I listened, my heart dropped for the guy. I began to feel sympathy for him, until he started expressing the reasons why he took this fight and how I was now the target of his hatred. I started to feel emotionally confused, but decided it was best to keep my game face on and keep this all business to myself. I didn't want him getting inside my head.

I looked up at him stoically from my seated position. Then he turned to look at me from the podium and said, "And that's why I'm knocking you the fuck out!"

I was completely taken aback. Things had just gone in a completely new direction, not to mention he put his fist in my face while saying it. What was I to do? This guy was pointing in my face with tears in his eyes over his son, while telling me he's going to knock me out in front of all my fans and the press of the Southwest. I obviously wanted to be classy about the situation, but fuck that. This was a fight and I needed to let him know that I would not tolerate his actions and that I would be sending him to join his son.

He now changed his small pity party to his own funeral. He shoved his nose into my face, taunting me. So, I did what any fighter would do and I knocked him the fuck out. No, wait. That's what went through my mind, but I couldn't risk the fight not happening. So I did the next best thing I could think of: I pushed him. I shoved him out of my face and launched him across the room. He jumped back at me, all hostile, and people from both our teams had to break us up while we both yelled obscene cuss words at each other.

The room was filled with anger and testosterone. The spectators scattered immediately. The whole front three rows moved back, behind all the cameras. Emotions were running high and I now felt a new hatred for him that I hadn't felt before. I was going to make him pay for trying to embarrass me in front of my family and my hometown. I was angry and I zeroed in on his plump, butterball belly. I knew my fist would penetrate the organs and ribs that were hiding, buried somewhere in his voluminous body fat.

Tensions were still high at the weigh-in, but they managed to keep us separated. I did my routine physicals and they kept having to take my blood pressure over and over. It was skyrocketing from my raging desire to kill this man. Finally they pulled me into a back room and calmed me down enough to take a reading that they could accept for the fight. After the weigh-in, I went home and got no sleep whatsoever. I just laid in bed fantasizing how I was going to hurt this man. I had to take a sixth Tylenol PM to finally calm down the adrenaline enough for me to fall asleep.

I got to the arena early to give me enough time to warm up and hit the hand pads with Herman. Herman wore a heavy body shield so that I could practice my exact timing on the body. We went over our body attack over and over. It was to the point that the penetration was going through the shield and hurting my trainer. My body shots felt crisp and clean, and I had mean intentions that night. We knew it would take just one of those good shots, and it would be *good night, motherfucker.*

As I entered the ring, there wasn't much of a crowd, maybe 2,500 people at most. We held the fight at NMSU, which was a forty-five minute drive for most El Pasoans. Still, that didn't faze me. I had come to fight and I was ready to kill this fucker. We got to the center of the ring and stared each other down. I could overhear some heckles from the crowd directed at his body. We looked at each other with hatred and then reluctantly touched gloves. I went back to my corner and knelt to say a prayer to God and to my late sister. I made the sign of the cross and popped up back on my feet. I turned around and waited for the bell. I was nervous, yet I was still filled with hatred.

The bell rang and he charged toward me to meet me in the middle of the ring. I wasted no time and I started jabbing his wrinkled forehead while setting up for the big body shot. He got even more brave than me and started throwing wild Hail Marys at my chin. He obviously had no game plan and was planning to go for broke. The crowd went wild. He caught me with a few shots, because his style was now in street-fighter brawler mode. I felt his punches sting me a bit. I noticed he didn't pack much of a punch, but they were enough to get my attention. I took a step back from his pressing action to collect myself. He charged at me again to claim dominance, and I saw him dip down exposing one of his many fat rolls. I saw my clean opening and BAM! I knocked the cheeseburger out of him. He went down in pain and took a knee. He barely got up at the count of eight, and I wasted no time on furthering my attack. I ran right back out to him and cracked him in the same exact spot like a whip. BAM! He went down, and this time he was rolling on the canvas with a twisted grimace on his face. He spit out his mouthpiece and yelled out a shriek of pain. The medics jumped in to see if he was okay and helped him to his feet. The referee lifted my hand in victory, and now I knew the Heavyweight Championship of the World was in my sights.

I was now 36-0 with thirty-four big knockouts. I was feeling unstoppable once again. I had secured my sixth professional title and I was awaiting a world title shot. I knew nothing could stop me except myself.

When that feeling of invincibility comes over me, that's when I'm at my most fearless—and at my most careless. I was now feeling fearless and the world was my oyster. It was time to go off and celebrate with the boys while I waited for that one big phone call for a title shot. I was like a powerful and fast-moving locomotive with no brakes, but I didn't know I was heading in the wrong direction. My life was about to make a turn that would change my course and direction forever.

CHAPTER 25

HELLO DEATH,
NICE TO MEET YOU AGAIN

WBC Heavyweight Champion of Mexico

've heard many stories of people that have died and came back. They see a bright light at the end of a tunnel and they get pulled through it. They feel the ecstasy and love of God, and they're surrounded by loved ones that have passed. It always sounds so amazing and wonderful. They almost always come back to this life in disappointment, wishing they could only return to God and what they refer to as "home." That's a thought I loosely hold on to in my mind as I write this.

The weekend after the fight I decided to head to Scottsdale, Arizona to celebrate the sixth championship and visit a good buddy of mine, Trader. He was a funny, charismatic type of guy and when we got together, all kinds of crazy would happen. We had the same exact birthday, only a year apart. We had met only a few years prior and we were already becoming great friends. We would laugh hysterically together about anything and everything, and when we went out, we always had our fun with the ladies. We were the perfect team for closing deals, and the deals were how many girls we could take home on any given night. I was a hunter and I was all about the kill. I often kept a particular souvenir of my victims and it only counted if they were given voluntarily. I could have given lace panties away as stocking stuffers for Christmas. I considered those items "kill trophies."

On that particular weekend, a few of the fellas from Dallas decided to fly in and meet us in Scottsdale to join the party. This one night started out like every other crazy party night did. We pre-raged at some unlucky bastard's house, leaving one helluva mess, then we jumped into two cabs to make our way to Old Town Scottsdale, where all the happening clubs were just kicking off. Excitement was in the air. I had just won my sixth heavyweight title and I was finally back in contention for a shot at the Heavyweight Championship Crown. My record was now 36-0 with thirty-five brutal knockouts, and I felt indestructible.

The air that night was crisp with a slight wind chill. I was still in great shape from the fight that past weekend. I wore a short-sleeved Western-looking shirt with stylish jeans and brown snakeskin cowboy boots. All I knew that night was that

I wanted to get my drinking game going strong, but fuck ever taking that GHB shit again. I was too smart for that. Drugs were not on my menu anymore. I just wanted some good old-fashioned fun with my buddies.

We bounced around the first few hours, hitting different clubs and bars, taking rounds of tequila shots at each one. I wanted to have my last shot at fun, because the year ahead of me was going to be a grueling and defining one that would pave my way to superstar status and success. I was nervous, yet I felt ready and willing to impress and shock the entire sports world. I was on a mission to upset and defeat the Klitschko brothers with stunning upset victories and to claim my mark in heavyweight boxing history forever.

After celebrating most of the night at different bars, we decided to land at a bar called "El Jefe" and to post up there until the end of the night. We had girls all over us. We had a table with multiple bottles and every girl in the bar was coming up to our table to see what the action and celebration was all about. There was this one girl in particular that made it a point to come and sit on my lap and flirt occasionally. She was gorgeous. We even ended up kissing a little. I noticed she started to get aggravated with all the other girls that were surrounding our table, so she pointed and told me, "I'll be over there, so now you know where to find me, okay, Champ?" I nodded in agreement and she went off in that direction.

As the night started to wind down a bit, I noticed she had found her way to a new group of black men to put her arms around. I didn't think anything of it, so we paid the bar tab and I began my way out of the bar. She yelled out, "Hey handsome! Are you going to an after party without me?" I turned around smiling and stumbled my way over to her. As I approached, I noticed the men looking me up and down, while making short comments under their breath. I knew it was negative, but I chose to ignore it. She was also showing obvious signs of being intoxicated. Before I could pull myself back to walk away, she reached up and put her arms around my neck and tried to kiss me. I kissed her a little and looked up to lock sight with a set of jealousy-driven eyes.

One of the men sitting there said coldly, "You should walk on outta here, playa."

I said back, "After you go fuck yourself, slick," and added my signature fuck you smile. She kept hanging all over me and kissing my neck. They all confidently stood up and stared at me. There was about four of them and they all stood at 6'1 to 6'2 in height. I moved the girl off me and to my side, because I was about to make extremely quick work out of all of them. I had already zeroed in on the first two men I was going to smash.

One of them spoke up and flexed his neck back tightly. "What up, playa? You think you wanna mess wit dis right here?"

I said, "Like taking candy from a baby."

Their eyes got wide. I stared at them without flinching. I was feeling my adrenaline flow, but they did nothing. At that pivotal and delicate point, a few of my friends came running back inside the bar screaming for me to come outside so we could all go to the after party. I began walking backwards with my eyes still locked in on them and made my way outside, where I pushed off the girl that was locked onto me and said, "Get outta here. You're causing fucking problems." She looked up at me with a face of disappointment and regret and stumbled her way back inside.

Outside I was starting to feel cold, nervous and ornery, so I decided I would grab a slice of pizza to calm my nerves, while beginning my three-mile walk back home to slumber. I left my friends without saying any goodbyes, stumbling in the direction of the pizza place so I could enjoy a hot slice on the cold walk back home. It was starting to drop in temperature even more, but screw it, I was drunk and completely oblivious to the outside elements.

As I drew nearer to the pizza place, I heard the sound of shuffling and footsteps behind me. Out of curiosity, I turned around to see what the commotion was. There they were again, the group of men from the bar.

All of them were looking me up and down, calling me names, "What up, you cracker-ass bitch? You gotcha yoself some beef?"

I walked arrogantly toward them and said, "No, but feel free if you do."

They all looked startled, and scattered as I approached even closer. After claiming my drunken dominance, I turned back around to stand in line for my pizza slice. I stood there, swaying back and forth, trying to keep my posture. I stared off into the distance in a trance, looking at a brightly lit-up orange and yellow neon sign that kept blinking on and off. I remember paying close attention to the moths that were racing back and forth with a sequenced kamikaze attack on the sign. It was as if I was being warned in the oddest of ways by nature itself. Next I felt a dark presence I will never forget.

I felt someone approach me on my right side, then on the left side. I could see a silver glare approaching my face from the left. I turned to look and RIP! I felt a piercing stab below my ear, followed by a vicious rip-tear through my jaw and throat. I immediately felt shock overtake my body and I took a step back. I was gazing at my attackers in horror as the blood gushed uncontrollably out of the base of my neck. I tried to catch the blood escaping my body with my stained and slippery hands. Blood poured through the spaces of my fingers as all hope left me. My vision blurred while my heartbeat slowed down, drawing out the seconds remaining in my life.

Panic hit me and I realized that I'd been murdered. I looked up at the faces of my assailants, but they had blurs for faces. My shirt, jeans and boots had a new pattern of dark red blood spreading all over the concrete. My senses began to dull as I heard one final shout, "Finish that muthafucka!"

Out of nowhere, my buddy Jess came running in on the confrontation from my left side. I knew that he saw the conflict, but I don't think he could have anticipated the use of a knife. I saw Jess throw his hands up in a horror of panic, guarding his chest and face. The violent thug lunged forward with the knife and began delivering killing thrusts at him, trying hit the areas Jess instinctively covered.

There was nothing I could do. I blacked out and my consciousness went from rolling cinema film to still pictures. I saw Jess staring, moving his lips in horror. "Oh my God, David, we gotta get to a hospital."

I will always remember his eyes, fixated in disbelief on my face and throat. My throat was literally hanging off of my jaw and the gash was at least 9 inches wide and 10 inches long. You could see every pulsing artery and vein from my left ear to my collar bone. Things went out of focus and started to get blurry again. I had no energy. I felt no more pain. I was light like the air. I saw a pair of woman's legs with high heels rushing up to me. I felt a wool scarf wrap around my face and neck with a thrust as someone tied a knot at the top of my skull. Then I heard the sound of an ambulance in the background as it drowned out all of the horrific screams and yells. I lost consciousness.

I woke up inside the ambulance. Through my blurred vision, I saw the paramedics frantically rushing and dropping medical instruments, covered from head to toe in my blood. I could feel the ambulance swerving, shifting and speeding around the traffic. One of the paramedics kept yelling at me, "NO NO NO. DON'T DO IT. DON'T YOU DO IT! STAY AWAKE!" As he was yelling at me, it all went quiet. I heard nothing. It became peaceful. Before I shut my eyes for the last time, I saw a tall, relaxed shadow standing to the left of me. It had human form, and it wasn't threatening. It was supposed to be there. I must have entered some kind of altered state of consciousness. I was only focused on the shadow. I started to trustingly embrace it. Then it grew bigger and bigger and even bigger.

Everything went black.

My childhood and adolescence appear as flashes on a movie screen across my mind. I'm floating over my casket, looking into my own vacant corpse. I have a small contented look upon my face. My poor mother is crying uncontrollably while my father holds her, consoling her. He's pale, piqued and sick-looking. He stares at my body, shaking his head in disbelief, asking why. My consciousness floats around a familiar cathedral and I realize it's St. Patrick's. I recognize it from my old private school. The colors are vivid and bright green. Brightly blossomed flowers are all around me. I look peaceful. I have no expression and I'm wearing a nicely tailored, blue pin-stripe suit. I realize then that I am dead. I start screaming, "Noooooooooo! Mom, no! I'm sorry! Please God, no! No, Mommy!! I'm so sorry! Dad!! Please, Dad, look at me! Dad!!! Please, God, why? No!!"

In the depth of this helplessness, I saw a bright, white light. It was blinding me. I could barely make out the sounds of the frantic direct orders and medical jargon. I could smell the smell of bleach. Upon awakening I looked around my unfamiliar environment and I noticed nurses scurrying all around me. The haze started to lift and the fog began to clear.

I looked over at one of the nurses, and she said, "It's okay, hon. You know where you are?"

I said, "Am I dead?"

She chuckled and said, "No, you're in the recovery room from surgery, sweetheart."

I was confused. I laid my head back down on my pillow and began contemplating what I had just witnessed. It was so surreal. I laid there, frozen, as the doctors and nurses readjusted my positioning.

After what seemed just a few moments later, one of the nurses came back into the room to take my vitals once again. She told me, "The doctor would like to see you now."

I was reluctant and confused but I slightly nodded okay. The left side of my face felt hot and swollen. The doctor walked in. He was a well-groomed, soft-spoken, delicate, intelligent Indian man. He said, "How are you feeling, Mr. Rodriguez?"

I responded, "I've seen better days, but I feel fine I guess."

He reached over to my chin and turned my face from side to side as he examined me, glasses tilted down. "Smile for me, will you?"

I did so. I started smiling and making stupid faces, until the swelling and the pain began to bother me. He said, "Amazing, no nerve damage."

I was confused. He started to walk out of the room, then he turned around and looked back at me to say, "Someone up there must be looking out for you, Mr. Rodriguez, because you should have died. At the very least, you should've had facial paralysis. I was also not supposed to be on call tonight. You just got lucky and got yourself one of best cosmetic surgeons in the world, son." He waved at me and continued his walk out. I laid my head back down and my eyes began filling with tears.

Moments later, with no warning, the nurse let my rowdy group of excited friends barge in. I wasn't prepared, nor was I in the mood. I was severely drugged up, but I decided to act positive, sober, and unfazed by the incident. I had to not show any vulnerability to my pack of wild dogs.

Rocky analyzed me and said, "Hey, let us take a look at it now that it's all sewn up."

Before I could decide or say anything, he pulled the bandage back and snapped a picture with his phone. He mass texted it to everyone he knew, especially girls. It went viral immediately. I felt completely violated and I wanted to get up off my hospital bed and kill him for it. I knew he meant well, but I was in a sensitive and vulnerable moment. I believe he just thought it was an amazing survival and needed to be documented.

"You didn't mind I took that picture, did you? It's gonna be a badass scar, bro!"

I was weak so all I could muster was a look of disgust and to lay my head back on the pillow. I had just been sabotaged, but I pretended it didn't bother me and I laughed it off with them. I didn't want to show any kind of weakness, but the truth was that I felt frightened, helpless, and confused.

They decided to give me my deserved peace to rest and left my room. I picked myself up and stumbled slowly into the bathroom to take my first look into the mirror. They had told me I had received 369 stitches inside and outside my face and throat. I knew I could never fully prepare myself for what I was about to view, so I decided not to further the agony and to muster up the courage to look in the mirror.

I removed the bandage and stared into a vast, unknown abyss in a state of paralyzed horror. I pushed myself away from the cruelty and knelt over the toilet and began crying uncontrollably. I felt violated, deformed and now mutilated. I felt like a humiliated child once again, but this time my face had been changed physically, and forever. My life would never be the same. I had never had anyone so deliberately and viciously try and take my life. I felt dirty and disgusted inside. It was an intimate action to use a knife to the face. I remember thinking that I would rather have been shot. It takes a very jealous and hateful person to do such an act of evil. I knew then that the scar on my face was going to damage me not only physically, but mentally and emotionally as well.

To this day, the assailants have never been caught. The media attacked me and treated me like a criminal instead of a victim. Since when does political correctness excuse a senseless act of attempted murder? Soon I would realize that they may not have succeeded in taking my life, but they had succeeded in taking my career.

CHAPTER 26

NOTHING CAN STOP ME

Okay, so I took a knife to my throat and face and almost lost my life once again. That still wasn't going to stop me from achieving my destiny as the Heavyweight Champion of the World. At least, that's what I was hoping, anyway. Looking back, I should have sought professional counsel and extensive therapy. I was definitely not in a healthy enough mental state to resume training and fighting again, but I had a championship to win and nothing was going to get in my way. I took the doctor's advice and let my face heal for six months. Let it heal just enough so that I can inflict more punishment on it in the ring—makes a lot of sense.

The newly added addition to my face took some time to get used to. The constant questioning and stares from strangers were the hardest to endure. My life was now completely different. Everywhere I went, whether it was the grocery store or a movie theater, I was always gawked at and treated differently. I was perpetually harassed. I began to grow accustomed to the routine stares and invasive questions.

The bravest questions always came from little children, who always seem to have a no-holds-barred outlook about life. They'd be the first to come out swinging with the questions: What happened to your face? What did you do to deserve that, sir? They were relentless, but I must admit they were cute. One kid even asked me if I could go with him to his "show and tell" to speak on survival to his class. Kids always had a way to lighten up my heavy situation. I couldn't tell them the real story, that I got knifed in the face by a group of thugs, so I would get a real kick out of telling them that I just nicked myself shaving. I loved watching the confusion set in on their little innocent faces as they would digest that sarcastic answer. It was the only real thrill I could get, having this freshly carved conversation piece on my face. I figured the least I could do is have fun with it. A newly added feature had made its lifelong home along the contour of my jaw line. Every time I looked in the mirror to shave or brush my teeth, I had an unfamiliar addition to my grin. It was a fresh, daily reminder of the vicious and senseless attempt on my life.

I felt as if I had been turned into the Joker from *Batman*, and I would now seek revenge on the world that had turned so cruel to me. At least, that's how I thought back then. Now I see the scar as something completely different. I see it as God's grace for sparing my life. A tough lesson of God's love. After almost dying twice in one year, I knew there had to be more for me to do on this three-dimensional plane of existence. In some crazy and spiritual way, almost dying twice had lifted my depression. I realized how fragile life really is, that it's a gift. I often reflect on this idea: It's not about the glass being half empty or half full, it's about the beauty of the glass itself.

My appreciation for life was setting in more and more every day, but I still wanted to finish my dreams of boxing.

Many people asked me why I would risk myself getting hurt any further, but I was on my own spiritual journey. It was my journey and I had to see it through the entire way.

After six months had passed, I decided to get back into the gym, get back into some hard work. I was out of the top fifteen in the WBC, but they were kind enough to put me on medical leave. I guess it's a nice gesture, holding my place in line out of sympathy. Still, I had to get back in the ring and make that big statement. I needed to prove that these clowns couldn't take my life or the career that I worked a lifetime for. Somehow I had to take back the dignity and self-respect that I felt I had lost.

As I was trying to overcome the trauma of the violent attack, I started to suffer from PTSD. Nights were the worst. Sometimes, when I was lying down, I would have flashbacks of the knife entering my face. I would feel a piercing pain strike my left side of my face and I would instantly jolt out of my bed to protect myself. This time of my life was the most awful and trying set of experiences to look back upon. As if almost getting murdered wasn't enough, I got served a lawsuit from my old team. Salami Slammer and Napoleon had decided to create a frivolous lawsuit, and to go not after just me, but after my family. My elderly parents were now the prime target of the hatred they had harbored for me. Salami and Napoleon understood that my family owned commercial real estate and they were absolutely bloodthirsty for it. They wanted their revenge and they would do anything and go through any measures to get it. Now my energy and focus was lasered in on them, instead of my all-important upcoming return fight.

I was training in Las Vegas, and I woke up every day full of anger and disgust that they would have the audacity to target my family. They had lowered themselves to the level of garbage just to get what they felt they were owed. They even paid a pathetic lowlife, jobless part-time sports writer to write a hate piece on me, just to fuel the flames before my upcoming fight. I had so much frustration and hatred brewing inside of me from the assault and now the lawsuit that my chest felt like an ocean of stormy and choppy water. I was never in any kind of peace at all. Some might think that kind of aggression would be ideal for a fighter, but it isn't. It's the opposite. To fight, you need your attention and focus set on the opponent, watching for any mistake, any opening. All your mental focus and energy must be delivered respectfully to the opposing gladiator, not yourself.

After six months of doing nothing, in the darkest place of my life, I was heavy. I was overweight and extremely lethargic. Training midsummer in the desert heat was killing me. The gym had no ventilation and a stale, odious heat to it.

There were, however, some nice additions to this new training camp. I was living in Lake Las Vegas with my friend David Urrutia. He was trying to get clean from a drug addiction and I was trying to achieve my life's dream in the worst mental state I've ever been in. Looking back, that wasn't such a great combination for an athlete's training camp. My investor put me in a beautiful house with a view overlooking the Las Vegas strip and lake. The house was tucked away, nestled in the mountains outside Las Vegas, and the views were breathtaking. Every other night, I had a beautiful new female come visit me, and David's only responsibility for living with me was to perform damage control. If I ever wanted a particular female to leave early, David and I had a well-rehearsed routine where David would come running up the stairs, bang on my door and yell, "LET'S GO CHAMP! Time to run those mountains!" I would get up in a hurry and tell the girl my trainer was pissed off and that she had to leave immediately. After a look of panic and confusion dawned on her face, we would escort her out, shut the door, and laugh our balls off while giving each other high-fives.

Our arrangement worked out wonderfully. There was never a dull moment living in that house. But the constant juggling of ladies, hard training, PTSD, and a lawsuit, combined with all of life's other little issues, was just too much for any person, and especially an elite athlete, to handle at one time. However, I don't think I could have pulled through it if it hadn't been for David living with me and giving me his support and friendship. I know I was a pain in the ass to deal with, but emotionally I was hanging on to life by just a thread. When I needed a friend most, he was there. I know that lessons are taught to us and that certain people are put into our lives at critical moments. It's up to you to take away the valuable lessons from each hardship you endure in life.

David and I had our routine. We would wake up early to a healthy breakfast, go train hard in the gym, come back to eat, rest, then run the mountain at night. I was training very hard and the heavy, dense desert air of Las Vegas was helping me knock off the lethargic pounds in record time. I came into training camp weighing in at a heavy 280 pounds and I got myself down to a good 260 pounds just three weeks before my first test back. Things were finally starting to look like they were back on track. I had just signed a contract with a new promotional company and the future was finally starting to look bright once again. They had originally scheduled me to fight a bigger and much taller fighter than myself, so I was training diligently with a clear strategy for how to beat the taller man.

After the next couple weeks I was down to the 250s—still not the weight I was used to fighting at, but it would have to suffice. I usually weighed in around 245-248 pounds by fight time and I had less than a week to go. I wasn't too worried, because we were using this fight as a kind of tune-up to pave the way for bigger and better fights. This particular fight was scheduled for NBC and would be televised live. Nothing was going to stop me from making my long-awaited statement to the world. I was going to be the biggest comeback story of all time. Everything seemed to be going as planned, until I received a phone call that changed the direction of my life once more.

As I was at home one night, watching film on my next opponent, I received a telephone call from my manager. "Dave, it's Greg. How are you holding up, champ?"

"I'm good," I told him.

He said, "Well, we got a minor problem. We need to find a replacement for your opponent. He's not taking the fight anymore. He just wants too much money." My heart dropped, but I didn't want all my training and bravado to go to waste. My only other option would be to wait until the beginning of the new year. I was impatient and in a hurry to prove my point.

After troubleshooting with him for the good part of twenty minutes, we agreed on a replacement solution: Darnell "The Ding-A-Ling Man" Wilson. In boxing terms, he was what you would call a journeyman or veteran, and he had a reputation for being a ferociously hard-hitting puncher. Most fighters at my level would not fight Darnell because he was considered too high-risk and could spoil anyone's hopes for a shot at the Heavyweight Championship. I didn't care, though. I wanted to fight and I wanted the fight to happen right now. It was time to put the horrible tragedy behind me and start shooting for gold again. No more sadness or sulking.

The fight was scheduled to be held in Atlantic City,

and I only had a week to adapt to Darnell Wilson's ferocious punching style. The whole training camp prior to this minor change-up, I was training to fight "inside" and cut off the ring. When you fight taller fighters, you don't box them, you slip and move to get inside their arm range and then you explode going up with your legs to launch your attack. It was a style I was accustomed to using, and I was damn good at knocking people's heads clear off their shoulders once I was in punching range. I assumed I would just use the same exact method to fight Darnell, who was the shorter man in this fight. I was already too close to the fight to try and change up any specifics. Darnell only stood about 5'10 and weighed around 240. I knew his plan of attack would be to come in at me with the same type of ferocious style that I had, but I knew that once he did, he would have no choice but to take one of my shots on the chin and then that would result in good-night, baby. At least, this is how I had it all planned out. But things don't always go as planned. The boxing gods would have other ideas.

When I flew into Atlantic City, it was overcast and drizzling rain. There was an ominous, depressing feeling about being there that I just couldn't shake. I was not comfortable there, and the new promotional team I was dealing with treated me indifferently. It was not a feeling I was accustomed to. Usually the chemistry clicks together and everyone is in good spirits. This time, the fight felt more like a job. It just didn't feel right to me.

Nothing went as planned from the beginning. Our luggage went missing, there was a screw up over our hotel rooms, nobody had food coupons, and everything was turning into a long treacherous hassle. Dealing with all these little mishaps while having my emotional energy zapped by press conferences and the weigh-in, I hardly found any time to catch up on my sleep from the exhausting trip. I caught a cat nap whenever we had any breaks between media commitments.

When the day finally came for the weigh-in, it was psychological warfare from the moment Darnell and I saw each other. Whenever we passed each other in line for delivering paperwork or seeing the doctor, we would check each other with a hard bump to each other's shoulders. We even would lock eyes from across the room with a blank stare of an intense, hateful, distaste for one another. The conversation between our eyes told each other, FUCK YOU, I'M GOING TO KILL YOU AND YOUR FAMILY, MOTHERFUCKER. It was pure hate and it was that intense. Once we lined up for the weigh-in, it was business as usual.

I tipped in on the scale at a heavy-but-ready 255. He was next up. I lingered in his personal space to check on his weight myself. I was curious because he was short, but extremely stocky. We call the scale the lie detector, because you can say you're in shape all you want, but when you weigh in, the scale is your honesty gauge. He weighed in at a good 240. I looked and nodded slightly in agreement. I knew he came in shape and was ready to fight. There was no way he took this fight on a week's notice, as they had told me. This motherfucker came ready and had to have known about this fight weeks beforehand.

The media told us to pose off for the cameras. We got into each other's faces and I looked down at him. I could tell he was strong. He was built like a powerful spark plug. He reminded me of an old junkyard dog that had seen his share of life-and-death battles. I studied the battle scars and lines of a hard life on his face. I saw his nostrils flaring with deep intakes of air as our eyes pierced each other's soul. We stared blankly at one another for what seemed an eternity, and then he took a long casual yawn and said under his breath, "I'm meaner than you are."

At that moment I realized something terrifying. I realized I wasn't as ferocious as I used to be, before the attack on my life. The old David would have smacked him across his head and head butted him. This new David that I was just getting to know didn't say anything. I looked away first, and began posing for the cameras. I had just committed my first cardinal sin as a fighter.

That night I could hardly sleep. I was a bundle of nerves and his fearless comment kept playing over and over in my mind, like a broken record. I had a gut feeling, deep down, that this was going to be a serious test. I laid awake that whole night, preparing my mind for the battle that was to come. As the seconds, minutes and hours counted down, I got no sleep. In the morning I realized that he had won the first battle, but the war was still far from over—it was just about to begin. The hours of the day ticked away agonizingly, just as they did when I was in middle school awaiting the schoolyard bully.

The bell rang for round one. We wasted no time feeling each other out. We met in the middle of the ring and went full speed. Both of us wanted this fight to be over by knockout. Blood was on both of our minds and our fists were our extensions to kill. BLAM BAM BOOM BAM! He caught me with four devastating, thunderous punches before we hit the first ten seconds of round one. I reeled with my back against the ropes and blood began flowing down the back of my throat. My nose started to swell and my left eye felt deflated. It closed instantly. I knew my eye socket had been badly broken. The whole time I was enduring the rest of his assault, I was just thinking that something was seriously wrong with my left eye. It felt as if the muscles had gotten detached. In the back of my mind I knew I had now entered a living nightmare. I knew I had to fight and fight hard.

His attack subsided when he ran out of breath and noticed I was still standing. I had now weathered the assault, but I knew in the back of my mind that I had received serious physical consequences. I fired back at him and connected with three of my own brand. BAM BOOM BAM! He just looked at me with a blank, unwavering stare and kept marching forward. I knew I was in for a long and brutal night. We relentlessly traded punches back and forth for the remainder of the round. Neither of us gave an inch of ground. Every time I tried to slow him down with a clinch or to find my range, he would slip out and away to land a few more bombs on my beaten face and ribs. There was no slowing this monster down. That night, he was there to prove a point. Every time I went back to my corner, I could see the look of concern and desperation on all the faces of my team. I couldn't understand the instruction they were giving me because my ear drum had been broken. My hands were swelling up fast inside my gloves as well. I was getting hurt by this man's punches, and now I was hurting myself when I threw my own.

The bell rang for the final round. We met back in the center of the ring. Neither of us had let up an inch. The series of fireworks that I saw every time he hit me ensued. My lungs were badly burning and my muscles were fatigued, but I kept on fighting. Deep down inside I knew that this fight had been an epic war of wills. I believed deep down that I might just edge out the victory and maybe even catch him with my signature punch. I still couldn't be too sure, so I went for broke. I put all my chips in for the game-winning pot. I decided to take an uncalculated risk and lunge in to throw my final set of clean, crisp punches to impress the judges.

Right as I was lunging forward, I heard one of the officials bang on the mat for the final ten seconds remaining. That's all

I remember. Everything went quiet. Nothingness. I laid still on my back, motionless, as I had done to countless fighters. I was now the recipient of a knockout blow. As I began to wake and come to my senses, I started to feel and hear once again. I realized I was on my back in a weird, slow-motion dream state. I looked up from the canvas at a blurry Darnell Wilson in mid-celebration, jumping up and down with an elated look of excitement.

I didn't understand what had happened. *What the fuck is this guy so happy about? Did I just...? Oh man, I did... Please tell me this isn't true, God. Don't let me go out like this.* The foreign idea flooded into my mind: I had just got knocked the fuck out.

A familiar and caring voice came to my left ear. Out of my one good eye, I could make out the silhouette of my trainer, Rafael Garcia, speaking softly and lovingly to me. He said, "Stay down, son. You're badly hurt." They all clamored around me and picked me up off the canvas. They dragged me over to the stool to take my vitals. As I sat there, I felt completely alone.

I listened with humility and shame as Darnell was declared the winner by a knockout. I'd never been on this side of the match for my entire professional boxing career. The undefeated kid just got beat. It was an upset. The promoters' wet dream had just got mollywhopped into next week. This was not supposed to happen. What did I do so wrong for God to punish me over the last two years? My whole life began running through my mind at warp speed. I had so many questions but no answers. I was supposed to be the champion of the world. I'm the "Pride of the 915" and I can't go out like this. I can't end my career on my back! But that's exactly what happened.

Then a strange feeling of relief and acceptance came flowing over my body. I stood up, reached out and gave Darnell a hug and pat on the back saying, "Good punch, champ." He answered, "Man, you almost had me out, like, five times! How come you didn't finish me?" I stood there in confusion and replied, "Fuck, you got a good poker face then, bro, because I never sensed it." We both chuckled and gave a sportsman's hug again. Two gladiators showing respect and love after an epic war.

There is something that happens to two people after a fight like that. You somehow get connected for life. Two souls, gifted by the boxing gods to deliver a spectacular and sensational performance. It's an artistic and beautiful dance between two brave and unrelenting gladiators. We had our moment in time for the whole world to see. We both showed the world courage and bravery of epic proportions. That's the feeling every great fighter lives for. You always want to go down in history by showing your heart and soul. That fight did that for the both of us. We earned our respect from the boxing world and that is something nobody can ever take away. I knew I had finally received my Purple Heart in boxing.

CHAPTER 27

LOST
————

My flight back home was quiet. It was a five-hour journey altogether and everything felt surreal. People stared at me on the plane as I held an ice bag to the newly stitched laceration over my left eye. Nobody asked questions. It was just known that I was badly hurt, physically and emotionally.

When I arrived back home in El Paso, there was no celebration or welcoming party. Nobody was there to greet me or ask for an autograph. For the first time in years I felt alone again. I was humiliated and beaten. Why did God bring me back from death twice only to humiliate and destroy me? Is this my Hell? I couldn't figure it out and it plagued my mind for months afterward. I wanted nothing to do with anyone. I just wanted to curl up in a fetal position and die. I tried going back to the boxing gym but I had no fighting will or spirit. I was a beaten man.

I imagined all my ex-teammates laughing and joking about me, calling me a fraud and a loser behind my back. My imagination went ballistic. My days began to get tiresome after the never-ending restless tossing and turning I would endure at night. If I did get any sleep, it was usually followed by hellish nightmares of the referee's voice echoing in my mind as he stood over me counting to ten. I knew I would either have to accept this humiliating defeat or it would send me into a spiral of depression, drugs and alcoholism. My days became a constant struggle of decision making, whether or not to put a gun to my cranium. It wasn't the fact that I lost, it was the fact that everything I had ever worked for had evaporated. My dreams had washed down the gutter like yesterday's rain. My purpose had now escaped from my grasp.

I now knew what it felt like to be my dearest sister, hopeless, helpless and with nowhere to turn. Now I understood why the only counsel she could receive was from the bottom of a vodka bottle. She wasn't a bad person for choosing that life—she was just hurt and needed to mask her pain. It was an education I received from the best teacher, experience. As bad as I wanted to sulk and cry at the neighborhood watering hole, I couldn't. There was still a small spark of faith and hope still left inside me. I couldn't break my parents' hearts and die the way my sister did.

After days of tasting the stinging defeat, I knew I needed to show my heart as a real fighter and that meant getting back up, even if I didn't want to. I had to rise above this occasion and give it one more shot. This was now a life test, and boxing was just the tool the good Lord was using to test my character and soul. I had to at least fight one more time to regain my courage and self-respect. So without giving it any more thought or myself time to heal, I scheduled another fight for El Paso not even six months later. I was determined to make my hometown of El Paso and my family proud again. I needed to get my revenge on the boxing world.

At this point, I hated the sport with a passion, and people needed to pay for the way I felt. Who, though? I couldn't even answer that question. My patience was running thin and I needed answers. Scheduling another fight was the only answer I knew. I decided that this time around I wouldn't train in Las Vegas around the vultures and bloodsucking leeches. I wanted to train in El Paso, to be close to my family for emotional and mental support.

My PTSD had worsened and my nights were now a constant struggle. I still believed that seeking counseling was the easy way out and being a man meant handling your hardships on your own. Recurring nightmares about the attempt on my life still haunted me, and now I had a whole new set of issues. I got knocked the fuck out and suffered humiliation, while ruining my once pristine, polished and perfect record.

Against all the advice and loving opinions from people who cared about me, I still decided to get back in the ring. We decided to try this again and to fight another seasoned journeyman. I was at a level that I couldn't fight just anybody in my hometown. He had to have experience and be a good and rugged test, to prove my comeback was legit for the critics. We decided to fight a strong and durable fighter from Africa. His name was Raymond Ochieng. For some reason, I wasn't at all that worried about him. He posed no real threat to me. What your eyes just read right there was the second biggest cardinal sin I ever made in boxing. Dangerously, I took my opponent too lightly. I really felt that once I hit him, it would be all she wrote and I was confident in my ability after watching him on film.

The night of the fight he was acting scared, erratic, and overly emotional. During the stare down, I noticed every detail. He had beads of sweat pouring down his forehead, and his lips were parched and bright blue. He had this extremely nervous energy about him, with eyes that looked as though they had nitrous oxide being pumped into the backs of them. He stood before me, staring through me as if something was behind me. I couldn't read his eyes or gauge his behavior. Before we touched gloves to go back to our corners, I heard him chant some cryptic African mumbo-jumbo as if he was throwing some kind of black magic curse on me. Even the referee looked at him, confused and startled. I went back to my corner to hug my trainer, believing I was about to make things right in my life again.

The bell rang and I was on my ass not even twenty seconds later. I wasn't completely knocked out, like I was with Darnell, but I was definitely in a confused and dazed state. As I was struggling to get back up, I could see the referee counting over me with his latex glove in my face, but I still couldn't shake the confusion. I heard the count of 3-4-5-6, and then that was it. He hugged me and waved off the fight.

It was over as fast as it had started. I stood up, quite wobbly and in utter disbelief. I couldn't believe it had happened again. I was defeated for the second time in a row. My comeback after the knife incident had become a living nightmare and I was a proven failure. As I walked out of the ring, a lady in the crowd shook her head back and forth in disappointment at me. She gave a thumbs-down signal as she laughed out loud. I put my head down in shame and closed my eyes. I put my hands upon the shoulders of my trainer and followed his body like a blind man's walking stick.

I knew I wanted no part of boxing ever again. I was destroyed. I made my way through the crowd of nasty comments and laughter into the dressing room to hang my head in shameful silence and solitude. I had that all-too-familiar feeling of being alone once more. As I stared into the darkness of my hands, I felt an arm come across my neck and I got pulled in for a hug. I looked up and away from my cuffed hands to see my father. He looked into my eyes and said, "Davy. Let it go, son." I grabbed onto my father for dear life and began hysterically bawling my eyes out. I was releasing years of built-up tension, hatred, and frustration. Everyone in my dressing room at that moment knew to leave, in order to give us our father and son moment of privacy and space.

As I felt my father hug and embrace me, I felt a calming peace come over my soul that I hadn't felt since I was a child. He looked at me and gave me one last pat on the back, and told me, "You don't need this boxing shit any more, son. You've run the race well and I'm proud of you." I gasped a sigh of relief and gave him one last strong and meaningful hug. Looking back, maybe that's all I needed to hear. Maybe I just needed those few heartfelt words of acceptance.

Right then I decided to walk out into the arena where the television cameras were being displayed. Reporters came frantically running toward me for comments. I knew the bravery I was going to have to muster up, so I said a silent prayer to God and stared directly into the first set of television cameras. It was if I was looking into the very depths of hell. I didn't waver in my decision and decided to stand firm. I lifted my chin up high and I decided to say the hardest and most real words of my entire life.

I said, "It's over. I'm done. I retire."

The room of reporters lit up and exploded in a frenzy. Nonstop questions and popping flashbulbs started reeling out from every direction. I shrugged my shoulders as I fought back the tears, making my descent back into the dressing room without looking back. I knew if I looked back, I would have turned into a pillar of salt and been blown away into the sands of time. I would have been tempted to become the sad fighting story we so regularly hear about. I didn't want to continue my quest and become that punch-drunk, deteriorated shell of a man mopping gym floors the rest of his life. I needed to take that leap of faith in that very moment and get my life's priorities in order. I knew God had a bigger plan for me, even if I couldn't see it.

Over the next few days the anticipation for what my new life could bring, and what the future could hold without boxing, began to get dim. I was sad without the sport, but the longing for it began to creep back into my life like a spider on a windowsill. I would find myself revisiting my trophy and Championship belt case with fleeting thoughts of yesterday. The joy I had once held and the triumphs each belt had given me were distant memories. They were each symbolic for the conquering of my fears and the destruction of my demons. I often gazed at the belts and wondered what it would feel like if I could just fit one more championship belt in that case. Boxing used to be the way I exorcised my demons. I didn't have that luxury anymore. What would I do? How would I live a "normal" life? What do normal people even do, if they're not training to kick the living dog shit out of somebody else who stands between them and their dreams? Do I get a nine-to-five job and go against everything I ever believed in and stood up against? Do I now willingly enter the matrix and surrender over the sovereignty of my soul?

The fear was paralyzing. I'd always been a respected fighter and champion, but I was now the fighter of yesteryear. The questions kept bombarding me relentlessly with no answers. What was I going to do now—go back to school and actually become a working stiff? Get a job digging ditches or scrubbing floors?

I felt lost, but there was one thing I'd learned going through my journey: Only God knows when he is done with me, and I have no say in the matter. He was about to reveal a bigger and more defining purpose. An arena of a different kind. The arena of changing souls by the hundreds and, soon, thousands at a time. God had to prepare me through struggle to get me to where I was going. He had to break the arrogant and prideful fighter in order to use him for something much greater. My answer came in the most unlikely of places.

CHAPTER 28

PURPOSE

The depression had now set into my life full force. I was stranded on a desert island in the middle of the ocean without a boat, a compass, or even the sun to give me a sense of hope. I had no grasp on the reality I was living and I was losing my faith fast. I felt like a used-up whore. It was all a hoax. The joke was on me. I said that I would never look back on the triumphs of my past, but I couldn't help it. I had nowhere to go and I had nothing to look forward to. I went from a superstar to a nobody, or worse, a failure, like a Superman that had lost all his powers and was now made to live out the rest of his life as a disabled mortal.

I knew the depression was engulfing me, like the shadow I witnessed at the moment of my death. I fought it every day, but the force was too strong. The demons were attacking me on all fronts. They knew I was now at my weakest point and ready to give up in this round of my life. I was now the beaten fighter just waiting for the final bell to ring. Suicide was an itch that I had the constant urge to scratch. My parents' hearts might miss me, but the pain and loss I felt was too overwhelming.

After a few months of this deep sorrow, my father began to see he was losing his only son to the dark abyss of depression. He knew that if I was going to get out of this alive, I needed to find a purpose for living once more. He started to request daily that I get into the gym. Not necessarily the boxing gym, but a fitness gym. He wanted me to go to a gym and start sweating out the months of alcohol that I was accumulating in my system. I knew they had had the horror of watching my sister die the same way. They saw me buying that same one-way ticket to a life of hell and an untimely death. After months of feeling unaccomplished and disgusted with myself, I decided to throw that one last punch at life and listen to my father.

So I joined a gym and began working out with the regular folks. It was an odd paradigm at first. I would see these big, 'roided-out, muscular men hop up and down while making faces of intense anger, only to lift a heavy set of weighted plates up and down repeatedly. This was not my world. I came from the school of the true and tested gladiators. I trained with the skilled and battle-tested champions of the world. Not once did I see the fighters in a professional boxing gym display this type of comical insecurity and behavior. As I would walk from machine to machine and squeeze in a set here and there, I sometimes would hear the whispers of comments. Some were positive and some were deeply hurtful. I learned to ignore all of them and pretend not to care, except deep down, I really felt a dagger pierce my heart every time I overheard a comment of distaste or disapproval.

During the weeks of going to the gym, I would always see this one guy. He would come up to me with an oversized grin and a charismatic laugh. He would approach me with the same routine every day. His hand would be up in the air as he walked toward me, gesturing to give him a high-five.

He would blurt out, "Hey Champ! What's up, big dawg? You made El Paso proud! We need you to help the kids of your city!" What the fuck did this guy mean, help the kids? I'm not St. David of El Paso. I was supposed to be a world champion, not Mother Theresa.

The routine went something like this: he would be across the gym, I'd see him, then accidentally make eye contact, then regret it. As soon as he saw me, I knew the moment was coming. The music from *Jaws* would play continuously in my mind as he approached closer and closer. There was no stopping this guy. I knew the moment was coming that I would have to take a break from my workout and entertain some spiritual bullshit about how I need to help the kids of El Paso.

After weeks of pretending to listen to this guy, I decided to schedule a new time to work out at the gym to avoid him. This worked out wonderfully until one day, as I was laying down on the bench press finishing a set, I heard "the laugh." It was the sound of, HE JUST SPOTTED ME. Since I was about to rack the weight, it was too late. Sal was standing over me with that infectious grin, still continuing on with his signature laugh. My jig was up, I was now cornered. I decided to surrender and speak with him as long as he held me hostage. He was determined to schedule an appointment for me to meet with him and his girlfriend on material for a future speaking engagement. He promised a nice home-cooked meal with some cold beers. All I had to do was hear the guy out. I decided there was no harm in this and I should at least pay Sal back for his impressive persistence. After all, I was a fighter. I found favor in his attributes of dedication and persistence. Since he worked so damn hard for my attention, I could at least give him my attention over the course of one lousy dinner.

When I arrived at his house, I was greeted with that same

wide smile at the door. He greeted me and introduced me to the household. I wasn't sure what to expect, so I spoke briefly with everyone and sat myself at the table. I started to feel much more relaxed and I started to enjoy the caring friendship they were offering me. They were truly kind people and I started to feel a sense of guilt for not giving Sal the respect he deserved. I guess it was truly just me retracting from any kind of social or productive environment. I had been unwittingly becoming an introvert.

The conversation had much laughter and good spirits until we started talking about what actually got me into boxing. I had an epiphany at that very moment about exactly why I started boxing. It was bullying. My self-realization then catapulted the conversation into many other leaps and bounds and twists and turns. I was having a self-awakening that I never had before.

As we started to finish up the conversation over the delicious meal of carne asada and cervezas, the topic of discussion took another turn. It was a turn that pulled at my heart strings and made me realize that my problems as a child and teen were actually very common and becoming a serious epidemic. I learned about Veronica's story. Veronica was Sal's very polite and hospitable girlfriend. She was the one that hosted and made the dinner at her house, and she had a heartache and tragedy of her own.

Veronica had a son named Sebastian who had recently passed away from experimenting with a new designer drug called "N-Bomb." Sebastian had suffered from severe and relentless bullying. His death was a direct outcome of how he chose to deal with his issues of being bullied. The theme was the same as mine, except I had boxing as an outlet and Sebastian had nothing but built-up frustration and anger. He didn't have an outlet or mentor to save his life. He was on his own, like so many of the kids today.

After hearing his story, it was like a bolt of lightning hit me. I saw the reason why I was at that very house at that very time. I was resonating with Sebastian's story. It was almost like he was there in spirit, pleading with us to not let him have died in vain. He wanted us to know that he wanted his death at least to count for something bigger and with a deeper purpose. Kids today feel so alone with no voice or parental guidance, so they find the most natural outlet in the form of drugs, violence, and suicide.

I knew just how turbulent and confusing the teenage years and young adulthood could often be, so I told Sal and Veronica my own story. We knew right then and there the importance of this meeting. I realized right then that Sal and Veronica were going to be an important factor for change, a blessing. I realized that it wasn't that he was actually obnoxious or annoying, it was that he represented the change that demanded growth and self-reflection. His proposal of helping children mirrored a light inside of me that I hadn't been ready to let out and let shine. It represented a possibility inside of me that would come with severe growing pains. I was also scared of changing my ways because I knew that if I spoke to His children, God would hold me accountable. I knew I was once again feeling like a coward, but I couldn't hide in the face of righteousness. This time God was calling me and I knew I couldn't turn my back on the very source and light that had helped me throughout my darkest of hells growing up. I knew I had a purpose, that I held a key to the lock of changing children's lives with my story.

After this meeting I drove home and spoke with my sister over the phone in New York. My sister had coincidentally taken

The new arena

notes on her last visit to El Paso. She wrote down all my experiences of the terrifying life I led, of being bullied and the ramifications it held. I asked her to please put together some kind of a PowerPoint presentation that I could show to children.

This is when things started to grow organically, with lightning speed. Within a few short weeks, I had a legitimate presentation rehearsed and ready to present. In just one month, I was captivating audiences with my story in a different arena. A place I promised I would never return. A place I hated with every molecule of my being. A place I had feared and resented since a child. I was now giving my presentations in packed gymnasiums and detention facilities across the city. I was in the very places I promised I'd never return to.

I was now standing before audiences of high school and alternative school students in the hundreds and thousands. I

Team Lucid Love   *A bullied child*

could look at every kid in the classroom or gymnasium and know exactly what they were feeling. I once stood in the center of a ring, in front of thousands of adults, battling to render another man unconscious. Now here I was standing in a suit in front of hundreds of kids, where my teachers once stood, fighting to help the victims of bullying. Now I was front and center sharing my story of triumph, tribulation and humiliation to the thousands that needed it.

A thought would sometimes crack me over the head like a falling cinder block: God has got a twisted sense of humor. I remembered all the jokes I used to play on my teachers. All the sick pranks I delivered, making their lives and jobs a living hell. The irony finally hit me. The final prank was on me, and God was the ultimate practical joker. I was now back in the very places I hated, but this time I wasn't standing in front of a class apologizing for a specific prank or one of my many rude disruptions. I was there in a suit, commanding a captivated young audience. I was there to share a story about a boy who himself was once bullied, beaten and humiliated, but still went on to become a six-belt and once-undefeated Heavyweight Champion of the roughest of all sports, boxing.

CHAPTER 29

ONE MORE TIME

It was during a question and answer session after a presentation that I started contemplating the comeback. A child no older than twelve years old raised his hand and asked, "Mister, if you're talking to us about not quitting, then why did you give up after only two defeats?"

I was stumped. I couldn't answer that question. I couldn't explain to a child that once a fighter starts his downward decline, it usually doesn't end well. Usually a fighter ends up badly hurt and severely brain-damaged, becoming a punching bag or used as an opponent for hungrier, up-and-coming fighters. That was just too much to explain to a class of twelve-to sixteen-year-olds. They wouldn't understand an explanation like that. They would want the hero story about the man that went out winning.

As I stood there, silent, the class started clapping and chanting for my comeback. I was left standing there humbled and speechless. These kids didn't want to hear about my defeats and challenges. They wanted to see me rise again and be the champion that I was deep down inside. At the end of the presentation, I turned to Sal for support, but he just looked at me with a serious stare. He said, "You heard it from them, but they're not the only ones that want to see you come back and do it." I stood there with my hands in my suit pockets, staring down at the ground. Could I attempt to go back for one last shot? Do I really feel like giving up my reborn life of eating what I want and socializing the way I want, to be traded in for months of isolation for training? Just to come back and do it one more time? This was going to take some serious contemplation and decision making.

That following weekend I decided to break away and head to Las Vegas to join a friend and MMA fighter, Nick Diaz, for some kick-boxing fights at the Hard Rock. I really only wanted to go so I could get out of Texas and gain some much-needed mental clarity. As we walked around the fight arena, people of all walks of life came out to greet Nick Diaz. They were starstruck over my friend. I thought to myself that it felt just like yesterday that I was at the center of this kind of madness in the boxing world. The thought of the attention was temporary and fleeting. I realized it was superficial and I didn't miss it.

As I stood beside Nick Diaz as he took photographs, I heard my name being yelled out from a far distance. "Hey Niño! David Rodriguez!" I looked around, wondering who this individual could be. I saw a hand raised from ringside. He stood up. It was a man that I recognized, but he looked a little older than I remembered. I stared at him in confusion while he proceeded to stand up and wave me to come to see him. I didn't want to be rude, so I politely made my way over to him, through the congested crowds of people that were trying to get a photo with Nick Diaz. When I finally approached him, he shook my hand with a solid and firm grip. He was a good-looking man with a stocky build who stood about 6'1.

I looked at him for a few seconds trying to place him. Then it hit me. This guy was Ivaylo Gostev, a well-known manager of many fighters and champions, one of whom was the ex-heavyweight champion of the world, Samuel Peter. He specialized in heavyweights. Only a very few managers in the boxing business know how to handle a heavyweight career properly. This guy knew just that, and he was damn good at it. He gestured me over to the back bar for a beer and asked to talk to me. I wanted to decline, but he seemed sincere and I couldn't turn down a nice cold free beer.

As we talked, he told me he was a supporter and big fan of my once-promising career. He told me that if he had handled my career, I would have been heavyweight champion of the world. Upon hearing this I just smiled, taking sips of my ice cold beer with an empty longing in my chest. I respectfully lied to him and told him that I was now happy and hated the sport of boxing. He held a slight smirk and nodded in agreement. He began speaking to me in a very friendly, passive and non-aggressive way. This was something I wasn't used to from any boxing promoters or managers; usually they are brash and confrontational. I told him some brief points about my failed story and he seemed to be very sympathetic and understanding. He showed a certain distaste for the boxing business as well that I found uniquely pleasing.

After our conversation, I looked at him one last time while shaking his hand and said, "Let me think all this through. I've got a lot on my mind." I took his card and walked away impressed, but still a bit skeptical. He seemed like a good guy, but the boxing game is full of snakes and wolves dressed as sheep. I had to really put thought into making any kind of comeback. This was not going to be an easy decision. The thought of trading in my social life for months of stressful, grueling training wasn't an easy pill to swallow and digest.

That night as I laid in bed, that child's one question kept relentlessly torturing my mind. It's as if I was being water-boarded by her innocent question about quitting. I laid there contemplating the comeback. I thought about my age and all my surgeries. I wasn't exactly the young, prospected, thoroughbred racehorse anymore. I was pushing 38 years old, and in boxing, I was already an artifact of the past. The hunger inside me was dying and I felt my body was being held together by duct tape and bubble gum. How am I going to pull this old, beat-up, classic hot rod out of the garage, dust it off, and race it at performance level once again? I couldn't even imagine what the training or the recovery time from the rigorous daily routine would entail.

After a few days of much thought and conversations with my parents, I came to the soul-searching conclusion that I couldn't live a life with regrets. I decided I would give it one last honest run. I had to answer the questions that I knew would later plague my mind. I had to at least leave my career with the dignity of a sensational win. Before thinking on it much longer, I picked up the phone and made an excited but hesitant call to Ivaylo Gostev. He picked up and I simply stated, "Let's go for this one last time." After a few moments of a silent break, he replied, "We will be waiting for you in Vegas."

After I hung up the phone, I leaned back and took a slow, deep breath. I knew exactly what was in store for me and this task wasn't going to be an easy one. Within a few weeks, I was packed up and on my way back to Las Vegas for one last shot at redeeming myself. This time, leaving for training camp wasn't accompanied by the excitement of embarking on a new life or the thrill of becoming a champion. I was no longer that young kid seeking out his identity by chasing glory to cement his name in boxing history. I was now simply embarking on a different and more mature journey. I was out to reclaim and rewrite the final ending of my heartbreaking boxing story. I was going to do this for the survivors of bullying. I was going to lead the kids by example and give them the happy ending we all desired. I wanted them to see me go out of my career as a true success story, not as someone who gave up in the face of unwanted circumstances.

I knew the odds would be against me. I was once that bright, shining prospect on the upswing and highlight of his career, and now I was the weathered and bitter veteran on his treacherous decline. I was that older fighter that I once promised myself I would never be. I had become the fighter that a younger David Rodriguez once would have used to test his polished skills so he could reach the next level. I would now be the stepping-stone to other hungrier and younger fighters for their bright and promising careers.

So I did what any fighter in my position would do. I flipped my mindset and decided to become the old, mean, rabid junkyard dog. My years of experience and mule-kicking punching power should be more than enough to get me past the toughest of tests and battles. Once I arrived in Las Vegas, I started training the very next day. I was running against Father Time and I knew the hourglass was running out of sand. I needed to get to work fast if I wanted this comeback to be a success.

Ivaylo put me up in a nice little condo by the air force base, to be away from the temptations of the nightlife on the strip. I began my training diligently, with laser focus. Every day I woke up, trained early in the boxing gym, and then ran four to six miles each night. By the second week of being in the hot and arid desert air, I had managed to bring my weight down to a strong 248 pounds. My religious and determined discipline was paying off quickly, and the pounds were melting off me rapidly.

After a few weeks of adapting to this new routine, we began to coordinate our sparring. We brought in some of the biggest and baddest, most experienced heavyweights in the Las Vegas area. This is where you learn if you truly measure up. All the bag work, mitt work, and shadowboxing doesn't mean anything if you're not able to utilize it inside the ring. This is truly where the men are separated from the boys. This was my first test to see if I could still measure up with today's younger and promising talent.

As I entered the first sparring session, ready to gauge my abilities, I surprised myself once again. Not only did I bloody up this man's face, but I completely took him to school with my newly sharpened boxing ability. My trainer Kenny Reilly had been religiously sharpening my defense and boxing ability for the last few weeks. I was on fire and my punches were as sharp as a knife.

In the weeks leading up to my sparring, Kenny had me slowing down a bit and paying attention to my defense while only throwing the exact punches that I wanted to place. We wanted to conserve energy while making every punch count with knockout power and authority. My days of fighting like a wrecking ball were over. I was now thinking and reacting like a savvy, technically seasoned boxer. I was sparring every day and I was out-boxing my sparring partners continuously. I didn't even come close to losing a single sparring session. I came out on top of every single sparring session with not even a mark on my face. I was looking the sharpest I had in years.

After months of training camp and grueling work, my body was now a well-oiled and tuned-up fighting machine. I had undergone the hard work of transformation into a fisted killer. I knew now was the time to line up a fight before we risked any kind of overtraining or injuries. After having a long, thought-out conversation with Ivaylo, we decided the time was now to pull the trigger. I was dealing with a minor back injury that was beginning to hinder me at the time, so the fight had to be now or never. Father Time wasn't going to be waiting around for me to heal 100 percent. Those days had passed and we all knew it. If I wanted my revenge, we had to move in for the kill now. Time was valuable and of the essence.

Ivaylo acted fast and made some calls to other promoters in the boxing community to find a spot on a show. He found an upcoming fight card located in Salt Lake City that fit our script perfectly. He negotiated with the promoter and they came to the decision to host my comeback fight. After four years of frustration and turmoil since the accident, I would once again be the main event.

The next phase of the plan was to sit down and have a conversation about who exactly would be the new challenge. After agonizing research and tedious decision making, we decided my first fight back would be against a risky and tough Brazilian cruiserweight. His name was Gilberto Gutierrez and he had a solid winning record of 23-4, with twenty-one big knockouts. He was tough, but he was moving up to the heavyweight division and we felt his frame would not be able to withstand my unrelenting assaults of powerful punches. I watched many hours of film on him and he reminded me of a Pucheta-style fighter. He knew how to hang in to make a difficult and tough fight while pleasing the crowd with his bullshit antics and clowning. This is not the type of fighter you want for a comeback fight, but I knew I was on point with my power punches and I knew I could crush through his smaller cruiserweight frame. My fighting instincts told me his body would be softer, due to moving up to heavyweight, and his feet would be slower. I knew my punches had a way of keeping fighters honest to their weight class.

After much negotiation, he formally accepted the challenge. The fight had now become a reality. It was scheduled for early November and we were just turning the corner of October to enter November. That familiar shot of adrenaline quickly pulsed through my veins while attacking my nervous system. It was something that I hadn't felt in close to two years.

I only had a couple of weeks left of October so I decided to pick up my training in desperation. I knew I was already ready for the fight, but once that adrenalin to fight hits you, there is no way of wanting to slow down your training. I was now officially in "the zone," as athletes would call it. I never slept deeply. I awoke multiple times throughout each night, feeling my body racing with adrenaline. My body was telling me it was time to fight. After years of fighting, your body knows when it's about to be battle-tested. It understands that it's about to be put in the line of fire, and your subconscious takes over. I began heading nightly to the local CVS just to buy a bottle of NyQuil to help calm my nerves and knock my insomnia out. I didn't enjoy downing the half bottle of NyQuil, but I'd rather be draggy the next morning than to train while sleep-deprived.

I trained with sprains, strains, aches and bruising, but the powerful adrenaline my body was pushing out masked my pain. I was obviously used to these kinds of aches and pains throughout the years of boxing, but this time I was training with a new set of aches and pains I had never had in my younger years. My knees, back and hands were destroying my will to break through the mental barrier. Every day after a training session it was the same monotonous and heartbreaking routine: an ice bath for twenty minutes, followed by a handful of ibuprofen, only to lie in bed with ice bags on my knees, back and hands until the next training session. I didn't even have the energy to cook myself a decent meal. It got to the point where a chocolate protein drink would be my only source for nutrition.

I was feeling pathetically beaten, and I realized I was now the aging fighter. That weapon, denial, was no longer fighting off the symptoms of mortality. Defeatist thoughts would creep into my mind as I lay on my bed, trying to bargain with Father Time. I would fall asleep while the ice bags melted into my mattress and pillows. I was now an aged gladiator looking for his last shot of desperate glory. I continued battling these aches and pains throughout the remainder of training camp.

During the very last week of training, my coach knew the pain I was in and started pulling in the reins to conserve my energy and promote healing. In the last week, you've done all the hard work. Resting now is crucial and becomes your most important asset. We started slowing down the pace immensely and began training for maintenance and recovery. All the hard work had now been done in the months leading up to the fight. Now it was time to rest and save my energy for my opponent's ribs and face.

When we flew into Salt Lake City, it was freezing. The scenery was beautiful, and snow covered the endless rolling mountains. I would stare out from my hotel balcony trying to capture any kind of peace of mind the scenery would give me. I was a nervous wreck, as I had been before all of my fights, but the scenery somehow put a calming ease to my anxious and troubled mind.

I knew I was once again at another juncture in my life. This time, I was making the decision to see my dream all the way through to the end, with no regrets. Win or lose, I was willing to accept the outcome and move forward with my life with a sense of honor and dignity. It takes one helluva man to come back from what I had gone through. The mere act of deciding to return to the fight was my happy ending of epic proportions. By not giving up, I was leading by example. I was showing the countless afraid and bullied kids to never, ever cower in the face of adversity. Even if you feel beaten and destroyed, there is always hope, and your weapon is faith. When you find yourself in the depths of hell, look up, for even the act of doing so will show Satan he has no power over your soul. Win, lose or draw, I had already won the spiritual fight. I had beaten the odds and faced down my demons once again.

Showing up wasn't enough, though. I wanted to knock this motherfucker into la-la land and leave him wishing he never took the trip from Brazil.

I arrived at the weigh-in like a caged tiger. I had four years of pent-up frustration and anger to release. I had years of unfinished business that I was about to unleash with my fists. This poor motherfucker just flew all the way from Brazil to feel my revengeful wrath. I was not going to let him go home without permanent damage from David Rodriguez to remind him daily of the mistake of accepting the fight with me. The stare-down at the weigh-in was like a lion staring at a gazelle, calculating the quickest way to devour his meal. I didn't look at him as an opponent, but as a helpless prey with no way out or way to escape. I knew he felt my eyes piercing his through his body into his soul. After the faceoff he reached out to shake my hand. He had just committed the sportsman's cardinal sin, and I ate it up. I declined, and I knew I had this motherfucker right where I wanted him. It was only a matter of time before I got to taste fresh blood again. I put my headphones back on to ignore the noise and the frenzy of the people clamoring to ask questions. I had no time for the media or the people gathering around me to kiss my ass and distract me from my mission at hand. I was in kill mode and I hated anybody who tried to penetrate my concentration. I was literally fighting for the ending of my boxing story. I was going to make sure I didn't fuck up any part of this chapter.

I went to bed that night as nervous as I had been before every other fight, but this time was different. There was a silent peace that laid still within my heart. I knew I had come a long way and done things in my life that young boys only dream about. I drifted off to sleep that night with an amazing sense of gratitude and love for God. I knew I was being allowed to see my dream through to the very end. I knew that somehow my life had been spared and that I was being given a second chance to make things in my life right again.

The next morning, I was ready. I did my normal routine of every fight day. I took an ice-cold shower to knock out the NyQuil hangover and brushed my teeth an obsessive five times that day. It was a nervous habit I developed in the amateurs and I was superstitious about it. Every hour on the hour I would venture into my bathroom to nervously brush my teeth. I would make sure my gums were cut and bleeding so I could taste the blood inside my mouthpiece during fight time. I needed the distinct taste of my own blood in my mouth before every one of my fights. I used to like to swish it around in my mouth as I patiently awaited the hours to tick away until fight time.

This time I purposely showed up a few hours early to the venue so I could warm up correctly and get myself mentally prepared to destroy another human being. As I went through the motions of my warm up with only minutes left until my entrance, a grin dawned on me from ear to ear. My coach asked, "What's the grin all about, son?" I replied, "I've already done it, coach. I know I've got this." As confusion ran overtook his wrinkled forehead, I just nodded at him with confidence. He answered back, "Well, let's go whoop that ass then, son!"

The doors swung open. The commissioner came in and signaled that the crowd was eager and ready for my long-awaited entrance. It was now time to begin the slow walk to the most brutal and honest place on earth.

As I took the slow walk to the ring, I couldn't hear anything. The echoes of the crowd were nonexistent. The lights of the ring drew closer and closer. Soon, I was eye-level with the second rope of the ring as the bright ring lights baked down upon my body. I took each step of the small ring stairway nervously and cautiously. I felt the heat from the bulbs above me as I began to enter the ring. I climbed through the ropes slowly, like a lion focused on his kill. I was ready not only to fight, but to kill and destroy this man. As I stood across from my prey, waiting for the bell, my mind became flooded with thoughts about my life. It was like the flashback that I witnessed before my death. Visions of childhood bullies and other terrifying images displayed like a fast-moving movie across my mind. Those dark and evil demons that tormented me were about to be exorcised one last time.

The bell rings. DING DING!!! We greet each other in the center of the ring. BOOM BAM BOOM! I feel my fist penetrate all the way through to his sternum. I felt his cruiserweight insides collapse around my fist. He's on the canvas within the first seven seconds. I run to the neutral corner so the referee can begin the ten count. I see my prey struggling, showing what's left of his heart as he scrambles to lift himself up. He's showing me he's game and willing to defend his life. I laser back in on his left ribs which he's painfully holding.

The referee signals for us to continue the fight. I walk patiently out to my opponent as he braces in a defensive position to weather the onslaught. BOOM BAM BOOM WHACK!! I hear his ribs crackle and break as my gloves

Final Bell   *Six Belts*

pierce through his body. He crumbles to the floor as he shrieks in pain and his face distorts.

That fast, it's all over. I'm looking down on my kill with fierceness and hostility. Out of nowhere a wave of calmness comes over my soul. I realize I have now exorcised the demons that have plagued my life for the last four years. A feeling of righteous justice had just been handed over to me. The fight is now officially over. Everything becomes quiet around me. I hear my sister's calming voice speak to me through the chants and yells of the crowd, "I'm proud of you, little brother."

The referee grabs my glove and lifts it over my head in victory. Through all the commotion, I hear the announcer announce my name as the winner once again. AND THE WINNER, NOW WITH A STUNNING RECORD OF 37 AND 2 WITH 35 KNOCKOUTS AND NOW 25 OF THOSE BIG KNOCKOUTS BY WAAAY OOOOF THE FIRST ROOOUND!!! DAAAAAAAVID ELLLL NIIINOOOO ROOOOOOODRIGUEZZZZZZZZZ!!!

I didn't jump up and down in celebration. I looked up and pleasantly grinned at my guardian angels in a thankful satisfaction. I said a quiet "thank you" to my sister and to my beloved Rocky. The boy that was once a troubled teenager had finally found his way through the trenches of life to feel like a king once again.

I don't know if I will ever feel victory like this again in my life, but I know I have tasted the bitter and the sweet. I've felt the cold darkness and felt the beautiful warmth of the sunshine. I've seen the tops of the highest of mountains and fallen face first in the deepest of trenches. I've succeeded at great lengths, but only after I have failed miserably. One thing always remains true. I never gave up. God bless.

ACKNOWLEDGMENTS

This book has taken me a lifetime to make, but only a few weeks to write. Thank you most of all to my mother. She is the one who sat me down as a child and taught me how to read. She always told me that someday my reading ability would take me places and become a very important asset. Mom, thank you for the unrelenting hours and faith that you put into teaching your son how to read. It has proven to be a priceless gem throughout my life. This book proves to be but a small manifestation of your countless hours of patience and love for me. Thank you from your only son, Davy.

ABOUT THE AUTHOR

After winning six championship belts, possessing a 36–0 undefeated record—thirty-four by first-round knock-out—and rated thirteenth in the world by WBC, twelfth by WBA, and fifth by IBA, David "Nino" Rodriguez was geared up for a world champion challenge. Then he crashed into a wall of death—an ethereal reality, a staggering demolition of his physical prowess and future—and his struggle to revive and recoup his identity began. His prior thirty-three years of zest for exploring and engaging in passionate combat had thrust him into many cultures throughout the world: South America, Europe, the Pacific Islands, and the Australian Outback. His driving force was the addiction to the win—the exhilaration of conquering a brutal opponent, the sweat and anxiety of chasing the "sweet science" of boxing, an obsession that began at age five and consumed him for thirty years.

During that time David simultaneously mastered an entertaining, dynamic speaking skill, and is now the director of Lucid Love, a non-profit organization dedicated to helping bullied kids. He is a speaker in demand for both student and adult audiences, a Red Carpet escort and presenter of awards in Hollywood, and a frequent guest on radio shows.

His understanding of and insight into the extremes of the human experience and drama comes from whole-soul commitment to physical combat, ministering to kids in hospital wards, helping the homeless, and twice greeting his own death. He speaks to the anxiety and depression experienced by victims of bullying, and to the abandonment of defeat. His readers become him, and are taken through his eyes and thought through the wild, daunting, nightmarish, and compelling excitement of living his experiences with him.

CPSIA information can be obtained
at www.ICGtesting.com
Printed in the USA
FSOW03n0348051116
26981FS